JHO 100시간 영어 시리즈 ⑤ 문법

JHO 100시간 영어 시리즈 ⑤ 문법

읽기만 해도
영어 문법이 잡히는

문법 없는 문법책

100시간이면 당신의 영어 운명이 바뀐다

서문

5시간만 투자하면 됩니다.
집중해서 세 번만 읽어 봅시다.
곧 영어 문장이 영어 그대로 들어오기 시작할 것입니다.

어떤 언어든 문법을 해결하는 가장 확실한 방법은 문법에 맞는 글을 많이 읽어 보는 것입니다. 그렇게 하면 억지로 암기하는 문법 지식이 아닌 **문법 감각**이 생겨납니다.

문법 감각이 생겨나면 암기를 하지 않아도 문법 시험 문제도 잘 풀 수 있습니다. 이런 방식의 학습은 문법 실력뿐만 아니라 단어 실력과 독해, 리스닝 그리고 스피킹과 작문 실력까지 키워 줍니다.

그런데 영어 문장을 많이 읽어서 문법 감각과 영어 실력 전체를 올리려 해도 초보자가 부담 없이 읽으며 문법 감각과 영어 실력을 올릴 수 있도록 만들어진 교재는 거의 없는 실정입니다.

이 책은 이런 현실적인 문제를 해결하기 위한 것입니다. **이 책은 암기하는 문법책이 아닙니다.** 반복을 통하여 자연스럽게 문법 감각이 생겨나도록 한 책입니다. 그리고 중학생 시험대비 교재로도 사용할 수 있도록 중학 수준의 중요 문법은 다 다루었습니다.

초보자도 읽기만 하면 단어 실력도 늘고 영어 문법 감각이 생겨나며 독해 실력까지 빠르게 향상할 수 있도록 세심하게 기획하였습니다. 따라서 기초가 약한 고등학생이나 대학생들도 교재로 사용할 수 있습니다.

이 책에서는 중학교 2학년 수준의 단어만 사용하였습니다. 그래서 비슷한 수준의 단어들이 무수히 반복해서 등장합니다. 따라서 단어 실력이 약한 분들은 몇 차례 읽는 것만으로도 몇백 개의 단어를 쉽게 익힐 수 있을 것입니다.

이 책은 단어 실력은 좋은데 **영어 독해 속도가 너무 느린 독자들**에게도 탁월한 효과가 있을 것입니다.

실생활에서 자주 사용되는 문장들로 구성하였기 때문에 독서를 마친 후에 소리 내서 읽으면 **스피킹 교재로도** 훌륭한 역할을 할 것입니다.

5시간만 투자해서 3번만 집중해서 읽어 봅시다.
전혀 다른 영어 세상이 보이기 시작할 것입니다.

목차

서문   04

책의 특징   08

책의 구성 및 학습 방법   10
    1. 시험 목적이 아니신 분   12
    2. 스피킹이 필요하신 분   17
    3. 작문이 필요하신 분   18
    4. 시험 목적이신 분   19

1장. 문장의 기본 형태   23
    [종합 이해]   30

2장. 인칭 대명사   33

3장. 시제   41
    [종합 이해]   62

4장. 부정문 의문문 명령문   67

5장. 비교   81

6장. 수동태   87

7장. 동명사   95
    [종합 이해]   100

8장. 부정사   103
    1. 명사 역할   104
    2. 형용사 역할   110
    3. 부사 역할   112
    4. be + to   122
    5. 원형 부정사   126
    6. 부정사의 의미상 주어   130
    7. for 목적격 (of + 목적격) to 부정사   130
    8. too ~ to   132
    [종합 이해]   134

9장. 분사   139

10장. 강조   155

11장. 가정법   167

12장. As   181

13장. 관계대명사   193
    1. Who   194
    2. Which   198
    3. That   200
    4. What   202

14장. 조동사   209
    [종합 이해]   218

15장. 5형식 연습   221

※ 부록 : 리딩 기록표   232

책의 특징

1 왕초보도 **영어 그대로 이해하는** 영어 문법책

영어 문장을 한국어로 해석하지 않고 영어 그대로 이해하며 읽어 나가는 능력이 빨리 생겨날 수 있도록 세심하게 기획된 문장들로 구성되었습니다.

2 **따지거나 외우지 않고** 영어 **문법** 기초 완성

따지고 외우기만 하는 영어 문법은 시험장만 떠나면 현실에서는 별 도움이 되지 않습니다. 스토리가 강한 문장을 반복해 읽음으로써 현실에서도 통하는 **영어 문법 감각**이 생겨날 수 있도록 하였습니다.

3 **읽기만 해도** 잡혀가는 영어 문법

문법 실력이 전혀 없는 사람들도 몇 차례 읽는 것만으로도 영어 문법 감각이 형성될 수 있도록 스토리가 있는 문장들을 패턴 형식으로 구성하였습니다.

4 읽기만 해도 **늘어나는 영어 단어 실력**

중학교 2학년 수준 이하의 단어들로만 문장을 구성하여 비슷한 수준의 단어들이 반복적으로 무수히 등장하여 초보들은 몇 차례 읽기만 하여도 몇백 개의 영어 단어 실력을 부담 없이 늘릴 수 있습니다.

5 독해가 느린 사람들의 해결책

단어 실력은 좋은데 독해가 느린 사람들은 단어에 대한 부담 없이 한국어로 해석하지 않고 영어 그대로 빠르고 정확하게 이해하는 능력을 아주 빠른 기간에 키울 수 있도록 하였습니다.

6 왕초보도 **문법, 작문, 회화, 시험을 한꺼번에**

기초 필수 단어가 무수히 반복되고 실제로 자주 사용하는 표현들로 이루어진 문장들이기 때문에 초보자의 작문용이나 스피킹 교재로도 손색이 없도록 하였습니다. 아주 기본적인 해설도 자세히 하여 **초등학생, 중학생들의 기본 문법교재나 서답형 작문 시험 대비용**으로도 사용할 수 있도록 하였습니다.

QR코드를 인식하거나 아래 주소를 입력하시면 수정사항을 확인하실 수 있습니다.

http://jho100.kr

책의 구성 및 학습 방법

영어 문법을 잘 지키는 글을 많이 읽음으로써 문법적인 감각이 생겨나면 별도로 영어 문법 공부를 하지 않아도 현재의 수능이나 토익의 문법 문제는 80% 이상이 해결되며 그 과정에서 단어 실력과 독해 능력도 향상됩니다.

시험 목적으로 영어 공부를 하는 경우 먼저 문법을 잘 지킨 좋은 문장을 반복해서 읽음으로써 단어 실력과 독해 능력까지 키우고 문법 감각을 익힙니다. 이후 기출 문제를 몇 번 풀어보고 틀리는 부분만 오답 노트를 만들어 공부함으로써 문법, 단어, 독해를 동시에 빠르고 쉽게 해결할 수 있습니다.

시험 목적이 아니라 영어 리딩 실력 향상이나 영어 리스닝, 스피킹 능력 향상이 목적인 경우에는 문법 공부를 할 시간에 문법을 잘 지킨 글을 많이 읽음으로써 단어 실력과 독해 능력을 쌓아가면서 문법 감각을 향상할 수 있고 회화능력의 기초도 더 튼튼히 할 수 있습니다.

그러나 초보자의 경우 자신의 수준에 맞는 영어 문장을 많이 접하는 것이 현실적으로 쉽지 않습니다. 영어 문장을 읽어 나가다가 단어 실력의 부족이나 기초적인 문법 감각의 부족으로 영어 학습을 포기하는 경우도 많습니다.

바로 이런 현실적인 문제점을 해결하기 위해서 빨리 기초 단어에 익숙해지면서도 기초적인 영어 문법에 대한 감각을 키우고 영어를 영어 그대로 이해하는 능력을 향상할 목적으로 이 책은 집필되었습니다.

책의 분량은 중학교 3년간 교과서 세 권의 본문을 합친 양과 비슷한 분량이며 단어는 가능한 중학교 2학년 수준 이내의 것만 사용하려 최대한 노력하였습니다. 중학 수준의 문법 중에서 중요한 문법은 다 다루었기 때문에 중학생이나 기초 실력이 약한 초보자가 학습하기에 부담이 없는 문장들로 이루어져 있습니다.

이 책을 3~5회독을 하면 시험 목적인 경우 중학교 3년간 영어 공부의 40% 이상, 시험 이외의 목적인 경우 사실상 중학교 3년간 영어 공부의 60% 이상이 끝난 것입니다.

불과 얼마 뒤 학습을 끝낸 다음에 느낄 희열을 위하여 맨 처음에 읽을 때부터 이 책 맨 뒤에 부록으로 있는 리딩 기록표의 구분대로 읽는 시간(몇 분 몇 초)과 이해도(70, 80, 90...처럼, 10% 단위로 기록)를 기록했다가 마지막 마무리 학습 때 다시 기록하면서 맨 처음의 기록과 비교해 보시기 바랍니다.

기록해 두었다가 꾸준히 학습한 뒤 불과 얼마 뒤에 비교해 보시면... 좋은 교재로 원리에 따라서 학습을 한다면... 정말 영어가 별거 아니구나... 영어가 그렇게 어렵지 않구나...라고 확신하시게 될 것입니다.

1. 시험 목적이 아니신 분

① 공통 사항

시험 목적이 아니라 실용 영어 실력을 위하여 공부하시는 분들은 문법 설명이나 문법 용어에는 너무 신경 쓰지 말고 이해 위주로 문장을 읽어 나가시기 바랍니다.

읽다가 문장이 잘 이해가 안 되는 부분만 1~2차례 더 읽으면서 책의 처음부터 끝까지 그냥 쭉 읽어 나가시기 바랍니다. 100% 이해가 안 되더라도 대부분 오래지 않아 해결될 것이니 너무 스트레스는 받지 마시기 바랍니다.

가능한 영어를 영어 문장 그대로 이해하려고 노력하되 한국어로 해석이 돼도 너무 신경 쓰지 마시기 바랍니다. 'I love you.'라는 문장을 맨 처음 접했을 때 우리는 모두 한국어로 해석했습니다. 그런데 초보라 하더라도 'I love you.'를 지금도 한국어로 해석하는 사람은 없을 것입니다. 이것이 반복의 힘이고 시간의 힘입니다.

처음 읽을 때는 한국어로 해석을 하느냐 마느냐 혹은 얼마나 빨리 읽느냐는 중요한 문제가 아니니까 크게 신경 쓰지 말고 100% 가깝게 이해하면서 읽어 나가되 부록에 있는 리딩 기록표에는 반드시 기록하면서 읽어 나갑니다.

중간에 해설을 보느라 걸린 시간도 크게 보면 리딩 시간에 포함된다고 할 수 있으니 해설을 보는 시간도 포함하여 기록합니다. 이후의 모든 리딩에서도 마찬가지로 읽을 때마다 리딩 기록표에 읽고 해설을 보는 시간도 포함하여 기록합니다.

한 번 읽어 나갈 때 조금 이해가 안 되거나 어렵게 느껴지는 부분이 있으면 그 부분을 표시하면서 읽어 나갑니다. 이때 조금 어려운 부분과 쉬운 부분이 섞여 있더라도 리딩 기록표의 구분대로 표시하시기 바랍니다.

② 쉽게 느껴지시는 분

(1) 처음부터 책의 끝까지 읽어 나간 후에 특별히 어렵게 느낀 부분이 없는 분은 너무 쉽게 느껴져서 다시는 읽고 싶지 않을 수준인 부분만 빼고 처음부터 끝까지 리딩 기록표의 구분대로 2회를 더 읽습니다. (한 챕터를 한 번 읽고 난 후에 다시 또 그 챕터를 한 번 읽고 나서 다음 챕터로 진도를 나가는 방식으로 읽습니다.)

두 번째 읽을 때는 바로 앞에 읽었던 것보다 최소한 10%는 더 빠르게 읽는다는 목표를 세우고 가능한 그 목표를 달성하려 노력하며 읽으시기 바랍니다. 읽을 때마다 리딩 기록표에는 반드시 기록하면서 읽어 나갑니다.

(2) 쉬운 부분도 포함하여 책의 처음부터 끝까지 가능한 한 빠르게 읽어 나갑니다.

어느 정도 기초가 있는 분들은 앞부분이 너무 쉽게 느껴지실 것입니다. 그러나 쉬운 부분이라고 무시하지 마시고 그 쉬운 부분을 마치 한국어를 읽는 기분으로 읽고 다음 진도를 나가면 자신도 모르게 영어를 영어 그대로 받아들이는 기초 훈련을 하고 있는 것입니다.

사실... 쉽다고 해도 그 쉬운 문장도 한국어처럼 영어로 편하게 말을 하거나 작문을 하지는 못하지 않습니까?

이미 두 번 이상 읽었고 같은 문법 사항들이 반복되니까 처음보다 훨씬 더 빨리 읽힐 것입니다.

그러나 처음보다 약간 빠르게 읽히는 것에 만족하지 말고 최대한 더 빠르게 읽으려 노력하며 읽어야 합니다. 그러다 보면 영어가 한국어 해석 없이 영어 그대로 이해되는 것 같은 느낌이 강하게 오기 시작할 것입니다. 그때야말로 더 집중해서 더 빠르게 읽으려 노력하며 읽어야 합니다. 물론 이때도 리딩 기록표에는 반드시 기록하면서 읽어 나갑니다.

(3) 3번 이상을 읽었고 영어 문장들이 영어 그대로 이해되는 것 같은 느낌이 들면 이것으로 이 책의 학습을 끝내고 본인의 수준에 맞는 그러나 어려운 느낌은 거의 없는 교재를 대략 5~10분 정도의 분량으로 나누어서 2회씩 반복하는 방식으로 계속 리딩을 해나가시면 됩니다. 그리고 점차 조금씩 교재의 수준을 올려 나가시면 됩니다. 이런 경우 4시간 정도면 이 책의 학습을 모두 마칠 수 있을 것입니다.

(4) 3번 이상을 읽었는데도 영어 문장들이 영어 그대로 이해되는 것 같은 느낌이 들지 않으면 이 책을 다시 더 볼 필요가 있습니다.

책의 맨 앞에서부터 책 전부를 다시 읽되 리딩 기록표의 구분대로 너무 쉬운 부분은 1회만, 너무 쉽게 느껴지지는 않은 곳은 2회씩 (그 부분을 한 번 읽고 다시 그 부분을 또 한 번 더 읽는 방식으로) 최대한 빠르게 읽으려 노력하며 책의 끝까지 읽어 나갑니다. 이때도 리딩 기록표에는 반드시 기록하면서 읽어 나갑니다.

(5) 마지막으로 너무 쉽게 느껴지지는 않았던 부분들(앞 (4)에서 2회씩 읽었던 곳)만 최대한 빠르게 1회만 읽습니다.

이것으로 이 책의 학습을 끝내고 어려운 느낌이 거의 없는 교재를 대략 5~10분 정도의 분량으로 나누어서 2회씩 반복하는 방식으로 계속 리딩을 해나가시면 됩니다. 그리고 점차 조금씩 교재의 수준을 올려 나가시면 됩니다. 이런 경우 4시간 정도면 이 책의 학습을 모두 마칠 수 있을 것입니다.

이때 주의할 점은 과거의 시험공부 습관으로 다음에 학습할 교재를 조금 어렵게 느껴지는 교재를 고른다면 영어를 영어 그대로 이해하는 능력은 영원히 얻지 못한다는 것을 명심하시기 바랍니다. 쉬운 교재에서 점차 수준을 높여가는 것이 오히려 훨씬 빠른 길이라는 것을 잊지 마시기 바랍니다.

③ 쉽게 느껴지지는 않는 분

(1) 처음 읽었을 때 조금 어렵게 느껴져서 표시한 부분만 2회씩 다시 읽습니다. (그 부분을 읽은 후에 바로 다시 그 부분을 읽은 후에 다음으로 진도를 나가는 방식으로 읽습니다.) 2회씩 읽었더니 쉽게 느껴지면 다음 챕터로 계속 진도를 나가고 2회씩 읽어도 만족스럽지 않으면 그 부분만을 바로 다시 한 번 더 읽고 다음 챕터로 진도를 나갑니다.

3회를 다시 읽었는데도 만족스럽지 않은 곳이 있어도 리딩 기록표의 구분대로 표시만 하고 그냥 다음으로 진도를 나갑니다. 이런 방식으로 끝까지 읽어 나갑니다. 이때도 읽을 때마다 리딩 기록표에는 반드시 기록하면서 읽어 나갑니다.

(2) 앞 (1)에서 표시한 곳이 있는 분은 그 부분만 다시 2회씩 반복하여 읽습니다. (그 부분을 읽은 후에 바로 다시 그 부분을 읽은 후에 다음으로 진도를 나가는 방식으로 읽습니다.) 마찬가지로 이때도 읽을 때마다 리딩 기록표에는 반드시 기록하면서 읽어 나갑니다.

(3) 이번에는 책의 처음부터 끝까지 빠짐없이 1회씩만 읽어 나갑니다. 단순히 읽어 나가는 것이 아니라 가능한 한 빠르게 읽어 나가려 노력하며 읽어 나가시기 바랍니다. 읽어 나가는 동안 여전히 조금 어렵게 느껴지는 곳이 있으면 마찬가지로 리딩 기록표의 구분대로 표시만 하면서 읽어 나갑니다.

(4) 비로 앞의 (3)에서 표시한 곳이 있으면 그 부분만 두 번씩 다시 읽습니다. 이때 특히 어려운 부분은 소리 내서 한 번 읽은 후에 눈으로 2회를 읽도록 합니다. (소리 내서 읽는 시간은 리딩 시간에서 빼고 기록합니다.)

이번에도 모르는 단어가 있으면 2~3차례 단어를 써보며 단어를 익히는 시간도 가지도록 합니다. 이때도 읽을 때마다 리딩 기록표에는 반드시 기록하면서 읽어 나갑니다. (영어 문장을 보는 시간과 해설을 보는 시간을 포함하여 기록하되 단어를 익히는 시간과 소리 내서 읽는 시간은 빼고 기록합니다.)

(5) 최종적으로 처음부터 끝까지 최대한 빠르게 읽으려 노력하며 한 번에 읽어 나갑니다. 한 번에 읽어 나간 뒤에 별다른 어려움이 없다면 이것으로 이 책의 학습을 끝내고 만약 조금씩 찜찜한 부분이 있다면 그 찜찜한 부분만 소리 내서 한 번 읽은 후에 눈으로만 다시 읽습니다. (소리 내서 읽는 시간은 리딩 시간에서 빼고 기록합니다.)

(6) 이것으로 이 책의 학습을 끝내고 본인이 보기에 조금 쉽게 느껴지는 교재를 골라서 대략 5~10분 정도의 분량으로 나누어서 2회씩 반복하는 방식으로 계속 리딩을 해 나가시면 됩니다. 그리고 점차 조금씩 교재의 수준을 올려 나가시면 됩니다.

이때 주의할 점은 과거의 시험공부 습관으로 조금 어렵게 느껴지는 교재를 고른다면 영어를 영어 그대로 이해하는 능력은 영원히 얻지 못한다는 것을 명심하시기 바랍니다. 쉬운 교재에서 점차 수준을 높여가는 것이 오히려 훨씬 빠른 길이라는 것을 잊지 마시기 바랍니다.

2. 스피킹이 필요하신 분

(1) 앞의 기본 리딩을 먼저 마칩니다.

(2) 신뢰할만한 분으로부터 영어 발음을 먼저 제대로 배웁니다. 제대로 된 영어 발음을 배우지 않고 스피킹 연습을 너무 오래 하면 한국인이나 한국에서 오래 산 외국인만 알아듣는 이상한 영어가 됩니다. 그때 가서 발음을 고치려 하면... 사실상 불가능에 가까운 도전을 하여야 할 것입니다. 수 없이 보았던 사실입니다.

처음에 제대로 배우면 영어 발음을 익히는데 그렇게 많은 시간이 걸리지 않으니 영어 스피킹을 하시려는 분들은 반드시 발음 먼저 제대로 배우고 스피킹 연습을 하시기 바랍니다. 이 충고를 가벼이 여기지 마시기 바랍니다.

배울만한 마땅한 분을 찾기 어려우시면 《JHO 100시간 영어 시리즈 ② 발음》 교재로 학습하시면 됩니다. 영어 학습 전반에 대하여 제대로 알고 싶은 분은 《JHO 100시간 영어 시리즈 ① 학습법》을 참조하시기 바랍니다.

(3) 이 교재에서 9장 중 분사구문편, 10장 전체, 12장 전체를 제외하고[1] 나머지 부분을 소리 내서 10번만 읽어 보시기 바랍니다. 그 결과는 본인 스스로도 믿지 않을 것입니다. 20번만 소리 내서 읽어 보시면 회화학원을 1년 이상 다닌 사람보다 훨씬 더 스피킹 실력이 좋아질 것입니다.

이 책은 문법, 리딩, 작문, 스피킹 실력을 동시에 높일 수 있도록 세심하게 기획된 책이라서 그렇습니다.

---

[1] 리딩 능력을 키우기 위하여 중요한 문법 사항을 모두 다루다 보니 해당 부분은 문어체적인 표현이 좀 들어가 있습니다. 이 문장들은 소리 내어 읽기에 아주 좋지는 않아서 제외하였습니다. 그 부분을 제외하고 스피킹 연습을 해도 님의 스피킹 실력은 매우 빠르게 늘어날 것입니다.

3. 작문이 필요하신 분

(1) 앞의 기본 리딩을 먼저 마칩니다.

(2) 리딩 기록표의 구분대로 각 부분을 음미하면서 1회 다시 읽습니다.

(3) 방금 읽은 그 부분을 한 문장씩 써나갑니다. 바로 외워지면 외워서 쓰고 바로 외워지지 않으면 보고 쓰시되 외워서 쓰는 부분을 늘리려고 노력합니다.

(4) 위의 (2)와 (3)을 반복하면서 책 끝까지 진도를 마칩니다.

(5) 만족스러울 때까지 (2)와 (3)을 반복합니다.

위에서 설명한 이 교재의 학습 방법을 지키며 학습해 나가신다면 이 교재가 여러분의 선생님 노릇을 할 것입니다.

처음에는 조금 답답해도 마음을 비우고 그러려니~ 하고 읽어 나가다 보면 조금씩... 조금씩... 영어가 영어 그대로 들어오고 영어 문법에서 점점 자유로워지는 것을 느낄 수 있을 것입니다.

자! 한국어로 따지는 것은 이제 그만!

이제부터는 영어를 합시다!

4. 시험 목적이신 분

① 공통 사항

시험 목적으로 영어 공부를 하는 중학생 혹은 기초가 약한 고등학생이나 토익 수험생은 앞으로도 계속 영어를 접하고 영어 수험서를 공부해 나갈 것이니 단어는 그냥 커닝만 하고 지나간다는 생각으로 모르는 단어는 눈으로 한 번만 보면서 읽어 나갑니다. 그래도 단어 실력이 많이 늘어날 것입니다.

다만 모르는 단어가 너무 많은 분들은 모르는 단어를 2~3회 정도만 쓰고 익히며 진도를 나갑니다. 비슷한 수준의 단어가 무수히 반복될 것이니 한 번에 모든 단어를 외우지 않아도 금방 단어 실력도 늘어날 것입니다.

조금 이해가 안 되는 부분이 있더라도 해설을 참조하면서 처음부터 이 책의 맨 끝까지 한 번에 쭉 읽어 나갑니다. 처음 읽을 때는 한국어로 해석을 하느냐 마느냐 혹은 얼마나 빨리 읽느냐는 중요한 문제가 아니니까 크게 신경 쓰지 말고 100% 가깝게 이해하면서 읽어 나가되 부록에 있는 리딩 기록표에는 반드시 기록하면서 읽어 나갑니다.

중간에 해설을 보느라 걸린 시간도 크게 보면 리딩 시간에 포함된다고 할 수 있으니 해설을 보는 시간도 포함하여 기록합니다. 이후의 모든 리딩에서도 마찬가지로 해설을 보는 시간도 포함하여 기록합니다.

한 번 읽어 나갈 때 조금 이해가 안 되거나 어렵게 느껴지는 부분이 있으면 그 부분을 표시하면서 읽어 나갑니다. 이때 조금 어려운 부분과 쉬운 부분이 섞여 있더라도 표시는 리딩 기록표의 구분대로 리딩 기록표에 표시하시기 바랍니다.

② 쉽게 느껴지시는 분

(1) 처음부터 책의 끝까지 읽어 나간 후에 특별히 어렵게 느낀 부분이 없는 분은 너무 쉽게 느껴져서 다시 읽고 싶지 않을 수준인 부분만 빼고 처음부터 끝까지 1회를 더 읽습니다. 이때도 리딩 기록표에는 반드시 기록하면서 읽어 나갑니다.

(2) 2회를 읽었으면 이번에는 쉬운 부분도 포함하여 책의 처음부터 끝까지 가능한 한 빠르게 읽어 나갑니다. 이미 두 번이나 읽었고 같은 문법 사항들이 반복되니까 처음보다 훨씬 더 빨리 읽힐 것입니다.

그러나 처음보다 약간 빠르게 읽히는 것에 만족하지 말고 최대한 더 빠르게 읽으려 노력하며 읽어야 합니다. 그러다 보면 책의 중간쯤에서는 영어가 한국어 해석 없이 영어 그대로 이해되는 것 같은 느낌이 오기 시작할 것입니다. 그때야말로 더 집중해서 더 빠르게 읽으려 노력하며 읽어야 합니다. 물론 이때도 리딩 기록표에는 반드시 기록하면서 읽어 나갑니다.

(3) 3번을 읽었고 영어 문장들이 영어 그대로 이해되는 것 같은 느낌이 들면 이것으로 이 책의 학습을 끝내고 다시 수험공부로 돌아가면 됩니다. 이런 경우 2~4시간 정도면 3회독을 모두 마칠 수 있을 것입니다.

(4) 3번을 읽었는데도 영어 문장들이 영어 그대로 이해되는 것 같은 느낌이 들지 않으면 다시 볼 필요가 있습니다.

책의 맨 앞에서부터 책 전부를 다시 읽되 리딩 기록표의 구분대로 너무 쉬운 부분은 1회만, 너무 쉽게 느껴지지는 않은 곳은 2회씩 (그 부분을 한 번 읽고 다시 그 부분을 또 한 번 더 읽는 방식으로) 최대한 빠르게 읽으려 노력하며 책의 끝까지 읽어 나갑니다. 이때도 리딩 기록표에는 반드시 기록하면서 읽어 나갑니다.

(5) 마지막으로 너무 쉽게 느껴지지는 않았던 부분들(앞에서 2회씩 읽었던 곳)만 최대한 빠르게 1회만 읽습니다.

이것으로 이 책의 학습을 끝내고 다시 수험공부로 돌아가면 됩니다. 이런 경우 3~5시간 이내에 5회독을 모두 마칠 수 있을 것입니다.

③ 쉽게 느껴지지는 않는 분

(1) 처음 읽었을 때 조금 어렵게 느껴져서 표시한 부분만 1회씩 다시 읽습니다. 다시 읽었더니 쉽게 느껴지면 다음 챕터로 계속 진도를 나가고 다시 읽어도 만족스럽지 않으면 그 부분을 바로 다시 한 번 더 읽고 다음 챕터로 진도를 나갑니다.

두 번을 다시 읽었는데도 만족스럽지 않은 곳이 있어도 리딩 기록표의 구분대로 표시만 하고 그냥 다음으로 진도를 나갑니다. 이런 방식으로 끝까지 읽어 나갑니다. 마찬가지로 이때도 읽을 때마다 리딩 기록표에는 반드시 기록하면서 읽어 나갑니다.

(2) 두 번을 다시 읽어도 만족스럽지 않은 곳이 있었던 분은 그 부분만 다시 2회씩 반복하여 읽습니다. (그 부분을 읽은 후에 바로 다시 그 부분을 읽고 다음으로 진도를 나가는 방식으로 읽습니다.) 마찬가지로 이때도 읽을 때마다 리딩 기록표에는 반드시 기록하면서 읽어 나갑니다.

(3) 이번에는 책의 처음부터 끝까지 빠짐없이 1회씩만 읽어 나갑니다. 단순히 읽어 나가는 것이 아니라 가능한 한 빠르게 읽어 나가려 노력하며 읽어 나가시기 바랍니다. 읽어 나가는 동안 여전히 조금 어렵게 느껴지는 곳이 있으면 마찬가지로 리딩 기록표의 구분대로 표시하면서 읽어 나갑니다.

(4) 바로 앞의 (3)에서 표시한 곳이 있으면 그 부분만 두 번씩 다시 읽습니다. 이번에는 모르는 단어가 있으면 2~3차례 단어를 써보며 단어를 익히는 시간도 가지도록 합니다. 이때도 읽을 때마다 리딩 기록표에는 반드시 기록하면서 읽어 나갑니다. (영어 문장을 보는 시간과 해설을 보는 시간을 기록하되 단어를 익히는 시간은 빼고 기록합니다.)

(5) 최종적으로 처음부터 끝까지 최대한 빠르게 읽으려 노력하며 한 번에 읽어 나갑니다. 한 번에 읽어 나간 뒤에 별다른 어려움이 없다면 이것으로 이 책의 학습을 끝내고 만약 조금씩 찜찜한 부분이 있다면 아주 쉬운 부분만을 제외하고 그 찜찜함이 없어질 때까지 책 전체를 반복하여 읽어 나가시기 바랍니다. 마찬가지로 이때도 읽을 때마다 리딩 기록표에는 반드시 기록하면서 읽어 나갑니다.

이것으로 이 책의 학습을 끝내고 다시 수험공부로 돌아가면 됩니다.

④ 중학생이나 고등학생인 경우

학교에서 문법을 배울 때마다 이 책의 해당 부분을 5차례 정도 소리 내서 읽고 작문 연습을 해보면 서답형 시험에 큰 도움이 될 것입니다.

PART 01.
문장의 기본 형태

01 주어 + 동사

I smile. You smile too. we all smile.
He smiles. She smiles. They all smile.
I run. You run too. We all run.
He runs. She runs. They all run.
I run fast. You run fast too. We all run fast.
He walks slowly. She walks slowly. They all walk slowly.
I come early. You come early too. We all come early.
Tom comes early. Mary comes early. The dog comes early. They all come early.

02 주어 + 동사 + 보어

I am happy. You are happy. We are all happy.
He is sad. She is sad. They are all sad.
I am a boy. You are a girl.
He is a student. She is a teacher.

03 ① 주어 + 동사 + 목적어

I like an apple. You like an apple. We all like an apple.
She likes an apple. He likes an apple. They all like an apple.

단어 및 숙어

all [ɔːl] 모든
apple [ˈæpl] 사과
come [kʌm] 오다
dog [dɔːg] 개(동물)
early [ˈəːrli] 일찍, 이른
fast [fæst] 빠른, 빠르게
like [laik] 좋아하다, ~같은
Mary [ˈmeəri] 메어리(여자 이름)
run [rʌn] 뛰다, 달리다
sad [sæd] 슬픈

slowly [ˈslouli] 천천히, 느리게
smile [smail] 웃다, 미소
student [ˈstuːdənt] 학생
teacher [ˈtiːtʃər] 선생님
Tom [tam] 탐, 톰(사람 이름)
walk [wɔːk] 걷다

해설

1형식 : 주어 + 동사

He smiles. She smiles.
그는 웃는다. 그녀는 웃는다.

주어가 3인칭 단수(그 사람, 그 여자, 그것...)이고 시제가 현재일 때는 동사에 -s 또는 -es가 붙는다.

I run fast. You run fast too. We all run fast.
나는 빨리 달린다. 너도 빨리 달린다. 우리는 모두 빨리 달린다.

2형식 : 주어 + 동사 + 보어

I am happy. You are happy. We are all happy.
나는 행복하다. 너는 행복하다. 우리는 모두 행복하다.

3형식 : ① 주어 + 동사 + 목적어

I like an apple. You like an apple. We all like an apple.
나는 사과를 좋아한다. 너는 사과를 좋아한다. 우리는 모두 사과를 좋아한다.

I love you. You love me. We love each other.
She loves him. He loves her. They love each other.

03 ② 주어 + 동사 + 목적어 + 부사구

Tom gives a book to me and Mary buys a flower for me.
Tom brings a pen to me and Mary gets a pencil for me.

04 주어 + 동사 + 간접 목적어 + 직접 목적어

I give you a gift. You give me a gift. We give each other a gift.
Tom gives Mary a gift. Mary gives Tom a gift. They give each other a gift.

I send you a letter. You send me a letter. We send each other a letter.

He sends her a letter. She sends him a letter. They send each other a letter.

Tom gives me a book and Mary buys me a flower.
Tom brings me a pen and Mary gets me a pencil.

단어 및 숙어

always [ˈɔːlweiz] 항상
angel [ˈeindʒəl] 천사
angry [ˈæŋgri] 화나다
bad [bæd] 나쁜
bring [briŋ] 가져오다
buy [bai] 사다, 구입하다
flower [ˈflauər] 꽃
for [fɔːr] ~을 위하여
get [get] 구하다, 가져오다, 갖다 주다
gift [gift] 선물, 타고난 재능

letter [ˈletər] 편지
Mary [ˈmeəri] 메어리(여자 이름)
pen [pen] 펜(필기도구)
pencil [ˈpensl] 연필
send [send] 보내다

each other [iːtʃ ˈʌðər] 서로

해설

3형식 : ② 주어 + 동사 + 목적어 + 부사구

Tom brings a pen to me and Mary gets a pencil for me.
톰은 나에게 펜을 가져다주었고 메리는 나에게(나를 위해서) 연필을 갖다 주었다.

여기서 to me, for me는 부사구이다.

4형식 : 주어 + 동사 + 간접 목적어 + 직접 목적어

I give you a gift. We give each other a gift.
나는 너에게 선물을 준다. 우리는 서로에게 선물을 준다.

05 주어 + 동사 + 목적어 + 목적 보어

I make you happy. But you make me sad. This makes me sad.
She makes me happy and he makes me happy too. They make me happy.

I call you a genius but you call me a fool. This makes me angry.
She calls him a genius and he calls her a genius too. This makes them all happy.

단어 및 숙어

all [ɔːl] 모든
angry [ˈæŋgri] 화나다
call [kɔːl] ~을 ~라고 부르다 /
부르다, 전화하다
fool [fuːl] 바보

genius [ˈdʒiːniəs] 천재
make [meik] 만들다
sad [sæd] 슬픈

해설

5형식 : 주어 + 동사 + 목적어 + 목적 보어

I make you happy. But you make me sad. This makes me sad.
나는 너를 행복하게 한다. 그러나 너는 나를 슬프게 한다.
이것이(앞의 두 문장의 내용) 나를 슬프게 한다.

I call you a genius but you call me a fool. This makes me angry.
나는 너를 천재라고 부르는데 너는 나를 바보라고 부른다. 이것이 나를 화나게 한다.

종합 이해

You are beautiful. You love me and you always make me happy. So I call you an angel. An angel is good.

Tom is ugly. Tom always walks fast. He hates me and he always makes me angry. So I call him a devil. A devil is bad.

She is beautiful. She always calls me a genius. So I love her. And I sometimes send her a love letter.

Tom is ugly but he always smiles. And he sometimes gives me a gift. So I like him. He likes me too.

Tom gives me a book and Mary buys me a flower. I mean, Tom gives a book to me and Mary buys a flower for me.

Mike brings me a pen and Jane gets me a pencil. I mean, Mike brings a pen to me and Jane gets a pencil for me.

단어 및 숙어

always [ˈɔːlweiz] 항상
angel [ˈeindʒəl] 천사
angry [ˈæŋgri] 화나다
bad [bæd] 나쁜
beautiful [ˈbjuːtifəl] 아름다운
bring [briŋ] 가져오다
buy [bai] 사다, 구입하다
call [kɔːl] ~을 ~라고 부르다 / 부르다, 전화하다
devil [ˈdevl] 악마
fast [fæst] 빠른, 빠르게
flower [ˈflauər] 꽃
genius [ˈdʒiːniəs] 천재
get [get] 구하다, 가져오다, 갖다 주다
gift [gift] 선물, 타고난 재능
hate [heit] 싫어하다, 미워하다
Jane [ˈdʒein] 제인(사람 이름)
letter [ˈletər] 편지

like [laik] 좋아하다, ~같은
make [meik] 만들다
Mary [ˈmeəri] 메어리(여자 이름)
mean [miːn] 의미하다
Mike [maik] 마이크(사람 이름)
pen [pen] 펜(필기도구)
pencil [ˈpensl] 연필
send [send] 보내다
smile [smail] 웃다, 미소
sometimes [ˈsʌmtaimz] 가끔
Tom [tam] 탐, 톰(사람 이름)
ugly [ˈʌgli] 못생긴
walk [wɔːk] 걷다

I mean [ai miːn]
무슨 말인가 하면, 다시 말해서(자신이 한 말을 다시 설명하거나 수정할 때 씀)

PART 02.
인칭 대명사

01 There is....

There is a pen on the desk. There is a pencil case on the desk. "Is there a pencil case on the desk?" "Yes, there is a pencil case on the desk."

There are erasers and ball point pens in the pencil case. "Are there erasers in the pencil case?" "Yes, there are erasers in the pencil case."

02 I my me mine

My parents are my mother and my father. I love my father and my mother. My mom loves me and my dad loves me, too. My grandfather loves me and my grandmother loves me, too. This is my eraser. I mean this eraser is mine. This is my ball point pen. I mean this ball point pen is mine.

03 You Your You Yours

Your parents are your mother and your father. You love your parents. You love your dad and you love your mom. Your grandfather loves you and your grandmother loves you, too.

단어 및 숙어

case [keis] 상자 / 사례
dad [dæd] 아빠
desk [desk] 책상
eraser [iˈreisər] 지우개
father [ˈfɑːðər] 아버지
grandfather [ˈgrændfɑːðər] 할아버지
grandmother [ˈgrændmʌðər] 할머니
me [miː] 나를, 나에게
mean [miːn] 의미하다
mine [main] 나의 것
mom [mɑːm] 엄마
my [mai] 나의

parents [ˈpeərənts] 부모
pen [pen] 펜(필기구)
pencil case [ˈpensl keis] 필통(연필 상자)
pencil [ˈpensl] 연필
you [juː] 너, 너희들 / 너를, 너에게
your [ˈjuər] 너의, 너희들의
yours [juərz] 너의 것, 너희들의 것

ball point pen [bɔːl pɔint pen] 볼펜
I mean [ai miːn] 무슨 말인가 하면, 다시 말해서

해설

There is.... ~에 있다.

I (주격 : 나는) my (소유격 : 나의)
me (목적격 : 나를, 나에게) mine (소유대명사 : 나의 것)

You (주격 : 너는, 너희는) Your (소유격 : 너의, 너희들의)
You (목적격 : 너를, 너에게, 너희를, 너희들에게)
Yours (소유대명사 : 너의 것, 너희들의 것)

That is your eraser. I mean that eraser is yours. That is your ball point pen. I mean that ball point pen is yours.

04 We Our Us Ours

Tom is my brother. Mary is my sister. We are siblings. Our parents say, "Your siblings are your brothers and sisters. Siblings must not fight with each other." We answer, "Don't worry. We are siblings. We don't fight with each other. We love each other." But... when our parents are out... kk.

We love our parents and our parents love us. They love us and they give us lots of things. Our grandparents love us, too. We have our own house. The house is ours. There is a car in the garage. The car in the garage is ours, too.

05 He His Him His She Her Her Hers

He likes her and she likes him. They like each other. He gives her a flower and she gives him a small gift. They give each other something.

단어 및 숙어

answer [ˈænsər] 대답하다
brother [ˈbrʌðər] 남자 형제(형, 오빠, 남동생)
eraser [iˈreisər] 지우개
fight [fait] 싸우다
garage [gəˈraːʤ] 차고
gift [gift] 선물, 타고난 재능
grandparents [ˈgrændpeərənts] 조부모(할머니와 할아버지)
her [hər] 그녀를, 그녀에게
hers [hərz] 그녀의 것
him [him] 그를, 그에게
his [hiz] 그의, 그의 것
kk 이모티콘, 한국에서 문자를 보낼 때 쓰는 ㅋㅋ와 거의 같은 의미임
lot [laːt] 많은
Mary [ˈmeəri] 메리, 메어리(사람이름)
mean [miːn] 의미하다, ~할 작정이다
must [mʌst] (조동사) ~해야 한다
our [ˈauər] 우리의
ours [ˈauərz] 우리의 것

out [aut] 밖으로, 외출중인
own [oun] 자신의, 소유하다
parents [ˈpeərənts] 부모
sibling [ˈsibliŋ] 형제 자매, 동기
sister [ˈsistər] 여자형제(언니 누나 여동생)
small [smɔːl] 작은
us [ʌs] 우리를, 우리에게
worry [ˈwəri] 걱정하다, 근심하다

ball point pen [bɔːl pɔint pen] 볼펜
be out [biː aut] 나가다, 집을 비우다
Don't worry [dount ˈwəri] 걱정하지 마
each other [iːtʃ ˈʌðər] 서로
lots of [laːts əv] 많은
our own house [ˈauər oun haus] 우리 자신의 집, 우리집 /
our own 우리 자신의
one's(= my, your, his, her, their) own : 자신의,
my own : 나 자신의, his own : 그 자신의

해설

We (주격 : 우리는) Our (소유격 : 우리의)
Us(목적격 : 우리를, 우리에게) Ours(소유대명사 : 우리들의 것)

when our parents are out. 우리 부모님들이 나가시면

He(주격 : 그는) His(소유격 : 그의)
Him(목적격 : 그를, 그에게) His(소유대명사 : 그의 것)

She(주격 : 그녀는) Her(소유격 : 그녀의)
Her(목적격 : 그녀를, 그녀에게) Hers(소유대명사 : 그녀의 것)

This purse is his purse. I mean this purse is his.
This wallet is his wallet. I mean this wallet is his.

That purse is her purse. I mean that purse is hers.
That wallet is her wallet. I mean that wallet is hers.

06 They Their Them Theirs

He walks and she walks. They walk together hand in hand. They are my neighbors. They are husband and wife. The husband loves his spouse and the wife loves her spouse, too. They love each other. They love their children. They love their siblings, too. They love their children and their siblings. So their neighbors like them so much. Of course, I like them, too. The house is theirs. There is a bicycle in the garage. The bicycle in the garage is theirs. There is a car in the garage. The car in the garage is theirs, too.

단어 및 숙어

bicycle [ˈbaisikl] 자전거
child [tʃaild] 아이, 어린이
children [ˈtʃildrən] 아이들
garage [gəˈrɑːʤ] 차고
her [hər] 그녀를, 그녀에게
hers [hərz] 그녀의 것
him [him] 그를, 그에게
his [hiz] 그의, 그의 것
husband [ˈhʌzbənd] 남편
mean [miːn] 의미하다, ~할 작정이다
neighbor [neibər] 이웃 사람
purse [pərs] 지갑
(주로 여성용 작은 돈 지갑이나 작은 핸드백)
sibling [ˈsibliŋ] 형제, 자매, 동기
spouse [spaus] 배우자(부인 남편)

their [ðeər] 그들의
theirs [ðeərz] 그들의 것
them [ðem] 그들을, 그들에게
together [tuːˈgeðər] 함께
wallet [ˈwɑːlit] 지갑 (주로 남자용으로 양복에 넣는 돈지갑)
wife [waif] 아내

hand in hand [hænd in hænd]
서로 손잡고, 손에 손 잡고
I mean [ai miːn]
무슨 말인가 하면, 다시 말해서
of course 물론
so much [sou mʌtʃ] 대단히, 그만큼

해설

They(주격 : 그들은) Their(소유격 : 그들의)
Them(목적격 : 그들을, 그들에게) Theirs(소유대명사 : 그들의 것)

They walk together hand in hand.
그들은 손잡고 함께 걷는다.

They are husband and wife.
그들은 부부이다. (남편과 아내이다.)

PART 03.
시제

01 현재와 과거 ① be 동사

I am a teacher now but I was a student a long time ago.
We are good men now but we were bad boys a long time ago.
You are a bad woman now but you were a good girl a long time ago.
He is a good teacher now but he was a bad student a long time ago.
She is beautiful now but she was ugly a long time ago.

Yesterday I was happy and you were happy, too. We were all happy yesterday.
Yesterday he was sad and she was sad, too. They were all sad yesterday.

A long time ago, I was a good student and you were a good student, too. We were all good students a long time ago.

단어 및 숙어

ago [əˈgou] 이전에
am [æm] / was [wəz] / been [bi:n]
are [a:r] / were [wə:r] / been [bi:n]
is [iz] / was [wəz] / been [bi:n]
men [men] (man [mæn] 남자의 복수) 남자들
sad [sæd] 슬픈
student [ˈstu:dənt] 학생
teacher [ˈti:tʃər] 선생님
ugly [ˈʌgli] 못생긴

woman [ˈwumən] 여자, 여성
yesterday [ˈjestərdei] 어제

a long time ago [ə lɔ:ŋ taim əˈgou]
오래전에

해설

시제에 따른 동사 형태

동사는 시점에 따라서 현재, 과거, 과거분사 세 가지 형태가 있다. 과거분사는 현재완료나 과거완료 그리고 수동태 등에서 사용된다.

현재와 과거

① be 동사
be 동사의 변화 : am [æm] / was [wəz] / been [bi:n]
be 동사의 변화 : are [a:r] / were [wə:r] / been [bi:n]
be 동사의 변화 : is [iz] / was [wəz] / been [bi:n]

A long time ago, he was a good teacher and she was a good teacher, too. They were all good teachers a long time ago.

01 현재와 과거 ② have

I have a book and you have a book, too. We all have a book.
She has a pencil and he has a pencil, too. They all have a pencil.
She had a pencil and he had a pencil, too. They all had a pencil.
Yesterday I had a flower and you had a flower, too.
We all had a flower yesterday.

01 현재와 과거 ③ 규칙동사

A short time ago, he walked slowly and she walked slowly, too. They all walked slowly a short time ago.

Yesterday I worked hard and you studied hard.

A short time ago I smiled and you smiled, too. We all smiled a short time ago.

A long time ago I liked you but you hated me. But we both love each other now.

단어 및 숙어

am [æm] / was [wəz] / been [biːn]
are [aːr] / were [wəːr] / been [biːn]
both [bouθ] 둘 다
is [iz] / was [wəz] / been [biːn]
flower [ˈflauər] 꽃
hard [haːrd] 열심히, 어려운
have [hæv] / had [hæd] / had [hæd]
가지고 있다, 소유하다
has [hæz] / had [hæd] / had [hæd]
가지고 있다. : have의 주어가 3인칭 단수
(he, she, it 등)이고 시제가 현재일 때
have 대신 has 사용
hate [heit] 싫어하다, 미워하다
pencil [ˈpensl] 연필

slowly [ˈslouli] 천천히, 느리게
study [ˈstʌdi] 공부하다
teacher [ˈtiːtʃər] 선생님
walk [wɔːk] 걷다
yesterday [ˈjestərdei] 어제

a long time ago [ə lɔːŋ taim əˈgou]
오래전에
a short time ago [ə ʃɔːrt taim əˈgou]
바로 얼마 전에
each other [iːtʃ ˈʌðər] 서로

해설

② have 동사
have의 주어가 3인칭 단수(he, she, it 등)이고 시제가 현재일 때 have 대신에 has를 사용한다.

have [hæv] / had [hæd] / had [hæd]
has [hæz] / had [hæd] / had [hæd]

③ 규칙동사
대부분의 동사는 동사의 현재 형에 -ed가 붙어서 과거형, 과거분사형이 된다.

01 현재와 과거 ④ 불규칙 동사

I come early now but I came late yesterday.
My father came late yesterday and my mother came late the day before yesterday.

과거 시제 이해

You were beautiful. And you loved me and you made me happy. So I called you an angel.

Tom was ugly. And he hated me and he often made me angry. So I called him a devil.

She was beautiful. And she often called me a genius. So I loved her. And I frequently sent her a love letter.

Tom was ugly but he always smiled. And he frequently gave me a gift. So I liked him.

단어 및 숙어

always [ˈɔ:lweiz] 늘, 항상
angel [ˈeindʒəl] 천사
angry [ˈæŋgri] 화난
before [biˈfɔ:r] ~ 전에, ~ 앞에
call [kɔ:l] ~라 부르다 / 전화, 전화하다
come [kʌm] come [kʌm] /
came [keim] / come [kʌm] 오다
devil [ˈdevl] 악마
early [ˈərli] 일찍, 이른
frequently [ˈfri:kwəntli] 자주, 흔히
genius [ˈdʒi:niəs] 천재
gift [gift] 선물, 타고난 재능
give [giv] / gave [geiv] / given [givn] 주다
hate [heit] 싫어하다, 미워하다

late [leit] 늦은, 늦게
letter [ˈletər] 편지
like [laik] ~같은, 좋아하다
make [meik] / made [meid] /
made [meid] 만들다
often [ˈɔ:fn] 자주
send [send] send [send] /
sent [sent] / sent [sent] 보내다
ugly [ˈʌgli] 못생긴
yesterday [ˈjestərdei] 어제

the day before yesterday
[ðə dei biˈfɔ:r ˈjestərdei]
그저께(어제 이전의 날)

해설

④ 불규칙 동사

일부 동사는 동사의 현재형, 과거형, 과거분사형이 불규칙으로 변화하는데 이러한 불규칙 동사는 모두 합하여 약 100개 정도 된다.

기본 동사 과거형 익히기 ① 현재형 문장

Today, I get up at 7 in the morning. I brush my teeth and wash my face. And then, I have breakfast with my family.

After breakfast I leave my house. I go to school with my friends. My school is not far from my house. So we don't take the bus. We walk to school. We arrive at school at eight thirty.

School begins at nine. I listen carefully in class. After school, I do my homework in the library. When I leave the library, I feel tired. I don't want to walk home. So I take the bus.

I come back home at six. My mother is in the kitchen. She sings a song. I think she feels good. I go to my room. I read a story book. My mother and my sister talk to each other. My mother speaks loudly. So I close the door. My father comes home. My mother tells me to have dinner. I get out of my room. And I go to the dining room.

단어 및 숙어

after [ˈæftər] ~후에
arrive [əˈraiv] 도착하다
begin [biˈgin] / began [biˈgæn] / begun [biˈgʌn] 시작하다
breakfast [ˈbrekfəst] 아침
brush [brʌʃ] 닦다, 솔
carefully [ˈkeərfəli] 주의 깊게
close [klouz] (문 등을) 닫다
dinner [ˈdinər] 저녁 식사
eight [eit] 여덟, 8
face [feis] 얼굴
feel [fi:l] 느끼다
homework [ˈhoumwərk] 숙제
kitchen [ˈkitʃin] 부엌 주방
leave [li:v] 떠나다
library [ˈlaibrəri] 도서관
loudly [ˈlaudli] 큰 소리로, 소란스럽게
sing [siŋ] 노래하다
six [siks] 여섯, 6
speak [spi:k] / spoke [spouk] / spoken [spoukn] 말하다
talk [tɔ:k] 말하다, 이야기하다
teeth [ti:θ] 치아
thirty [ˈθərti] 30, 삼십
tired [taiərd] 피곤한
wash [wa:ʃ] 씻다.
with [wið] ~와 함께, 같이
yesterday [ˈjestərdei] 어제

after breakfast [ˈæftər ˈbrekfəst] 아침 식사 후에
and then [ænd ðen] 그리고 나서
arrive at [əˈraiv æt] ~에 도착하다
at eight thirty [æt eit ˈθərti] 8시 30분에
brush teeth [brʌʃ ti:θ] 이를 닦다
come back [kʌm bæk] 돌아오다
dining room [ˈdainiŋ ru:m] 식당
far from [fa:r frʌm] ~에서 멀리
feel tired [fi:l taiərd] 피로를 느끼다, 피곤하다
get out of [get aut əv] ~에서 나오다, 떠나다
get up [get ʌp] (잠자리 등에서)일어나다
have breakfast [hæv ˈbrekfəst] 아침 식사를 하다
have dinner [hæv ˈdinər] 저녁 식사를 하다
in class [in klæs] 수업 중에
not far from [na:t fa:r frʌm] ~에서 멀지 않은
sing a song [siŋ ə sɔ:ŋ] 노래를 부르다
story book [ˈstɔ:ri buk] 이야기책, 동화책
take the bus [teik ðə bʌs] 버스를 타다
talk to [tɔ:k tu:] ~에게 이야기하다

해설

I listen carefully in class.
나는 수업을 잘 듣는다, 수업시간에 집중해서 듣는다.

When I sit at the table, my father smiles at me. I see his face. He looks tired. We have dinner together.

After dinner, I go back to my room. I read the story book again. Two hours later, I feel sleepy. I stop reading the book. It is already 11 o'clock. I go to bed early.

기본 동사 과거형 익히기 ② 과거형 문장

Yesterday, I got up at 7 in the morning. I brushed my teeth and washed my face. And then, I had breakfast with my family.

After breakfast, I left my house. I went to school with my friends. We didn't take the bus. We walked to school. We arrived at school at eight thirty.

School began at nine. I listened carefully in class. After school, I did my homework in the library. When I left the library, I felt tired. I didn't want to walk home. So I took the bus.

단어 및 숙어

after [ˈæftər] ~후에
again [əˈgen] 다시, 한 번 더
already [ɔːlˈredi] 벌써
begin [biˈgin] / began [biˈgæn] / begun [biˈgʌn] 시작하다
brush [brʌʃ] 닦다, 솔
carefully [ˈkeərfəli] 주의 깊게
didn't [didnt] did not의 줄임말
do [duː] / did [did] / done [dʌn]
early [ˈərli] 일찍, 이른
face [feis] 얼굴
got [gat] get [get] / got [gat] / got [gat] 받다, 가져 오다
have [hæv] / had [hæd] / had [hæd] 가지고 있다, 소유하다
leave [liːv] / left [left] / left [left] 떠나다
library [ˈlaibrəri] 도서관
look [luk] 보다, ~처럼 보이다
nine [nain] 아홉, 9
o'clock [əˈklɑːk] 시(한 시, 두 시 할 때)
sleepy [ˈsliːpi] 졸린
smile [smail] 미소, 웃다
teeth [tiːθ] 치아, 이빨
tired [taiərd] 피곤한
take [teik] / took [tuk] / taken [teikn] 잡다, 가지고 가다

wash [waːʃ] 씻다
go [gou] / went [went] / gone [gɔːn] 가다
yesterday [ˈjestərdei] 어제

after breakfast [ˈæftər ˈbrekfəst] 아침 식사 후에
after dinner [ˈæftər ˈdinər] 저녁 식사후
and then [ænd ðen] 그리고 나서
arrive at [əˈraiv æt] ~에 도착하다
go back to [gou bæk tuː] ~로 돌아가다
go to bed [gou tuː bed] 자다, 잠자리에 들다
have breakfast [hæv ˈbrekfəst] 아침 식사를 하다
in class [in klæs] 수업 중에
look tired [luk taiərd] 피곤해 보이다
sit at [sit æt] ~에 앉다
smile at [smail æt] ~을 보고 미소를 짓다
story book [ˈstɔːri buk] 이야기책, 동화책
take the bus [teik ðə bʌs] 버스를 타다

I came back home at six. My mother was in the kitchen. She sang a song. I thought she felt good. I went to my room. I read [red] a story book. My mother and my sister talked to each other. My mother spoke loudly. So I closed the door. My father came home. My mother told me to have dinner. I got out of my room. And I went to the dining room.

When I sat at the table, my father smiled at me. I saw his face. He looked tired. We had dinner together.

After dinner I went back to my room. I read [red] the story book again. Two hours later, I felt sleepy. I stopped reading the book. It was already 11 o'clock. I went to bed early.

단어 및 숙어

again [əˈgen] 다시, 한 번 더
already [ɔːlˈredi] 벌써
come [kʌm] / came [keim] / come [kʌm] 오다
close [klouz] (문 등을) 닫다
dinner [ˈdinər] 저녁 식사
face [feis] 얼굴
feel [fiː] / felt [felt] / felt [felt] 느끼다
get [get] / got [gat] / got [gat] 받다, 가져 오다
have [hæv] / had [hæd] / had [hæd] 가지고 있다, 소유하다
kitchen [ˈkitʃin] 부엌 주방
later [ˈleitər] 후에, 나중에
look [luk] 보다, ~처럼 보이다
loudly [ˈlaudli] 큰 소리로, 소란스럽게
o'clock [əˈklɑːk] 시(한 시, 두 시 할 때)
read [riːd] / read [red] / read [red] 읽다, 독서하다
sing [siŋ] / sang [sæŋ] / sung [sʌŋ] 노래하다
sit [sit] / sat [sæt] / sat [sæt] 앉다
see [siː] / saw [sɔː] / seen [siːn] 보다
six [siks] 여섯, 6
sleepy [ˈsliːpi] 졸리는, 졸린
smile [smail] 미소, 웃는 얼굴
song [sɔːŋ] 노래, 지저귐
speak [spiːk] / spoke [spouk] / spoken [spoukn] 말하다
table [ˈteibl] 테이블, 식탁
talk [tɔːk] 이야기하다, 말하다
think [θiŋk] / thought [θɔːt] / thought [θɔːt] 생각하다
tired [taiərd] 피곤한, 지친
together [tuːˈgeðər] 함께, 같이
tell [tel] / told [tould] / told [tould] 말하다
two [tuː] 둘
go [gou] / went [went] / gone [gɔːn] 가다

after dinner [ˈæftər ˈdinər] 저녁 식사 후
come back [kʌm bæk] 돌아오다
dining room [ˈdainiŋ ruːm] 식당
get out of [get aut əv] ~에서 나오다, 떠나다
go back to [gou bæk tuː] ~로 돌아가다
go to bed [gou tuː bed] 자다, 잠자리에 들다
have dinner [hæv ˈdinər] 저녁 식사를 하다
look tired [luk taiərd] 피곤해 보이다
sing a song [siŋ ə sɔːŋ] 노래를 부르다
sit at [sit æt] ~에 앉다
smile at [smail æt] ~을 보고 미소를 짓다
story book [ˈstɔːri buk] 이야기책, 동화책
talk to [tɔːk tuː] ~에게 이야기하다

02 완료형 ① 현재완료 (have, has + 과거분사)

I have just finished my homework and Tom has just finished his homework, too. So we play together. (완료)

I am a Korean. But I have visited England once. And I have been to France twice. Of course, I live in Korea now. (경험)

He lived in France. But he came to Korea three years ago. And he has lived in Korea for three years. He lives in Korea now. (계속)

She had two pencils yesterday. But She has lost a pencil. So she has one pencil now. (결과)

Tom came to Korea two years ago and he lived in Korea. But he has gone to France. He lives in France now. (결과)

해설

완료형
① 현재 완료 : 과거의 어떤 시점에서 현재까지 있었던 일들의 동작이나 상태를 나타낸다.
의미상으로 굳이 구분하면 1) 그 일이 끝났음을 강조하는 완료의 의미(완료), 2) 어떤 일이 있었다는 것을 강조하는 경험의 의미(경험), 3) 현재까지 계속되어 왔음을 강조하는 계속의 의미(계속), 4) 과거의 일이 현재까지 영향을 미치는 것을 나타내는 결과의 의미(결과)로 구분할 수 있으나 그 의미가 명확히 구분되지 않을 때도 많아서 이러한 의미상의 구분은 현실에서 영어를 사용할 때는 별로 중요하지 않다. 또 이런 의미상의 구분은 이제는 중학교 모의고사나 중학교에서 보는 시험 외에는 시험에 출제되지도 않는다.

단어 및 숙어

ago [əˈgou] (얼마) 전에
came [keim] come [kʌm] /
came [keim] / come [kʌm] 오다
die [dai] 죽다
England [ˈiŋglənd] 영국
finish [ˈfiniʃ] 끝내다, 마치다
France [fræns] 프랑스
gone [gɔ:n] go [gou] /
went [went] / gone [gɔ:n] 가다
homework [ˈhoumwərk] 숙제
just [dʒʌst] 막, 방금
Korean [Kɔːˈriən] 한국인
know [nou] / knew [nju:] /
known [noun] 알다
lose [lu:z] / lost [lɔ:st] / lost [lɔ:st]
잃어버리다
month [mʌnθ]
(12달 중 한 달의 기간을 나타냄)달, 개월
once [wʌns] 한 번
pencil [ˈpensl] 연필

read [red]
read [ri:d] / read [red] / read [red]
읽다, 독서하다
three [θri:] 셋, 3
together [tuːˈgeðər] 함께, 같이
twice [twais] 두 번
two [tu:] 둘
visit [ˈvizit] 방문하다
year [ˈjiər] 1년(기간)
yesterday [ˈjestərdei] 어제

have been to [hæv bi:n tu:]
~에 가본 적이 있다
have gone to [hæv gɔ:n tu:]
~에 갔다(~에 가서 여기에 없다.)
live in [liv in] ~에 살다
of course 물론
play together [plei tuːˈgeðər]
같이 놀다

따라서.... 중학교 학교 시험을 준비하는 목적으로 문법 공부를 하는 것이 아니라면 완료, 경험, 계속, 결과 등으로 그 의미를 구분할 필요 없이 그냥 과거의 언제부터 현재까지 무슨 일이 있었다는 의미 정도로 이해하면 충분하다.

I have just finished my homework 나는 막 숙제를 끝냈다. (완료)
She has lost a pencil. 연필을 잃어버렸다. (그 결과 그 연필이 없다.)
He has gone to France. 프랑스에 갔다. (그 결과 여기에 없다.)

02 완료형 ② 과거완료 (had + 과거분사)

I had read the book. So I returned the book to the library. (완료)
She had seen me before. So she recognized me right away when she saw me yesterday. (경험)
He had been sick for three months and he died at last. (계속)
She had gone to France and she lived there. (결과)

03 진행형 ① 현재 진행형 (am, are, is ~ing)

"Hi, Mike. It's Tom. What are you doing?"
"Oh, Tom. Can I call you later? I'm driving now."
"OK. call me later. I'll wait for your call."

Billy is walking along the street. And he is thinking about his future. Meanwhile, Jane is driving down the same street. And she is thinking about her future, too. Meanwhile, Tom is walking along the same street, too. Then, where will they meet?

해설

② 과거완료 : 과거의 어떤 시점에서 과거의 또 다른 시점까지 있었던 일들의 동작이나 상태를 나타낸다. 의미상으로 완료, 경험, 계속, 결과로 구분할 수 있다.

So she recognized me right away when she saw me yesterday.
그래서 어제 나를 보았을 때 나를 바로 알아보았다.

단어 및 숙어

along [əˈlɔːŋ] ~을 따라서
Billy [ˈbili] 빌리(남자 이름)
call [kɔːl] 전화하다, 전화 / ~라 부르다
drive [draiv] 운전하다
France [fræns] 프랑스
future [ˈfjuːtʃər] 미래, 장래
gone [gɔːn] go [gou] /
went [went] / gone [gɔːn] 가다
ill [il] 아픈, 병든
Jane [dʒein] 여자 이름
last [last] 지난
later [ˈleitər] 후에, 나중에
library [ˈlaibrəri] 도서관
meanwhile [ˈmiːnwail] 한편, 그동안
meet [miːt] 만나다
Mike [maik] 남자 이름
month [mʌnθ]
(12달 중 한 달의 기간을 나타냄)달, 개월
once [wʌns] 한 번
read [riːd] / read [red] / read [red] 읽다
recognize [ˈrekəgnaiz] 알아보다
return [riˈtəːrn] 돌려주다.
same [seim] 같은
see [siː] / saw [sɔː] / seen [siːn] 보다
sick [sik] 아픈, 병난

street [striːt] 길, 거리
three [θriː] 셋, 3
wait [weit] 기다리다
what [waːt] 무엇, 무슨

at last [æt last] 결국
at once [æt wʌns] 즉시, 동시에
drive down [draiv daun]
운전하다, 운전해 가다
have been to [hæv biːn tuː]
~에 가본 적이 있다
I'll [ail] I will의 줄인 말
I'm [aim] I am의 줄인 말
for three months [fɔːr θriː mʌnθs]
세 달 동안
have gone to [hæv gɔːn tuː]
~에 갔다(~에 가서 여기에 없다)
right away [rait əˈwei] 즉시, 곧
think about [θiŋk əˈbaut]
~에 대해 생각하다
wait for [weit fɔːr] ~을 기다리다
walk along the street
[wɔːk əˈlɔːŋ ðə striːt]
길을 걷다, 길을 따라서 걷다

진행형

① 현재 진행형 (be ~ing) : 현재에 어떤 일이 진행 중임을 강조할 때 사용한다.

It's Tom. What are you doing? 나 톰이야. 너 뭐하니?
OK. call me later. I'll wait for your call. 그래. 나중에 전화해. 나는 네 전화를 기다릴 거야.
Meanwhile, Jane is driving down the same street. 한편 제인은 같은 길에서 (차를) 운전하고 있다.
Then, where will they meet? 그러면 그들은 어디에서 만나게 될까?

03 진행형 ② 과거 진행형 (was, were ~ing)

I was looking down the street last night. Then, you were walking down the street. Meanwhile, Tom was walking up the same street, too.

03 진행형 ③ 미래 진행형 (will be ~ing)

Please call me tonight. I will be waiting for your call.

He checked everything and then he went to bed early last night. He will not change his mind. He will be leaving this town this afternoon. I'll be missing him.

단어 및 숙어

call [kɔ:l] 전화하다, 전화 / ~라 부르다
change [tʃeindʒ] 바꾸다, 변화하다
check [tʃek] 점검하다, 체크하다
down [daun] 내리다, 아래로
everything ['evriθiŋ] 모든 것, 무엇이나 다
ill [il] 아픈, 병든
last [last] 지난
leave [li:v] 떠나다
meanwhile ['mi:nwail] 한편, 그동안
mind [maind] 마음, 정신
miss [mis] 그리워하다, 놓치다
please [pli:z] 제발
same [seim] 같은
street [stri:t] 거리
tonight [tu'nait] 오늘밤
town [taun] 도시, 읍
wait [weit] 기다리다

went [went] go [gou] /
went [went] / gone [gɔ:n] 가다

and then [ænd ðen]
그리고 나서, 그런 다음
last night [last nait] 지난 밤, 어젯밤
look down [luk daun] 내려다 보다
this afternoon [ðis æftər'nu:n]
오늘 오후
wait for [weit fɔ:r] ~을 기다리다
walk down the street
[wɔ:k daun ðə stri:t]
걸어 내려가다, 걸어가다(내리막길을 걷거나 멀어져 가는 것을 묘사)
walk up the street
[wɔ:k ʌp ðə stri:t] 걸어 올라오다, 걸어오다(오르막길을 걷거나 까까이오는 것을 묘사)

해설

② **과거 진행형 (was, were ~ing)** : 과거의 어떤 시점에 진행 중임을 강조할 때 사용한다.

Then, you were walking down the street.
그때 너는 길을 걸어 내려오고 있었다.

③ **미래 진행형 (will be ~ing)** : 미래의 어떤 시점에 진행 중임을 강조할 때 사용한다.

He will be leaving this town this afternoon.
그는 오늘 오후에 이 도시를 떠날 것이다. (떠나고 있을 것이다.)

I'll be missing him.
나는 그를 그리워할 것이다. (나는 그를 그리워하고 있을 것이다.)

03 진행형 ④ 현재완료 진행 (have been ~ing)

She didn't call me untill now. So I have been waiting for her call for three hours. I hate her.

He became a middle school student a month ago. He has been learning English for four weeks. And he has been reading the same book over and over again.

03 진행형 ⑤ 과거완료 진행 (had been ~ing)

He had been sitting on the chair for five hours. Then his back started to hurt. So he went out an hour ago. And he has been walking along the street since then.

He had been learning English for four years. But it was difficult. So he gave up English last year. But he decided to study English again a month ago. And he has been reading the same book over and over again since then.

해설

④ 현재완료 진행 (have been ~ing)
과거부터 현재까지 어떤 일이 계속 진행되어 왔음을 강조할 때 사용한다.

So I have been waiting for her call for three hours.
그래서 나는 그녀의 전화를 3시간 동안 계속 기다렸다. (기다려 왔다.)

단어 및 숙어

again [ə'gen] 다시, 또
ago [ə'gou] 전에
along [ə'lɔ:ŋ] ~을 따라서
back [bæk] 등, 허리/ 뒤쪽
call [kɔ:l] 전화하다, 전화 / ~라 부르다
chair [tʃeər] 의자
decide [di'said] 결정하다
difficult ['difikəlt] 어려운, 곤란한
five [faiv] 다섯, 5
four [fɔ:r] 넷, 4
hate [heit] 싫어하다, 미워하다
hour ['auər] 시간
hurt [hərt] 아프다, 다치다
last [last] 지난
learn [lə:rn] 배우다
middle ['midl] 중앙의, 한복판의
month [mʌnθ] 달, 월
same [seim] 같은
since [sins] ~이후, ~이래로
sit [sit] 앉다
start [sta:rt] 시작, 시작하다
street [stri:t] 거리
three [θri:] 셋, 3
until [ən'til] ~ 할 때까지
wait [weit] 기다리다
walk [wɔ:k] 걷다

week [wi:k] 주, 일주일
go [gou] / went [went] / gone [gɔ:n] 가다

a month ago [əmʌnθ ə'gou] 한 달 전에
an hour ago [ən 'auər ə'gou] 한 시간 전에
decide to [di'said tu:] ~하기로 결심하다, ~하기로 결정하다
for five hours 5시간 동안
for four weeks 4주 동안
for four years 4년 동안
for three hours 세 시간 동안
give up [giv ʌp] 포기하다, 그만두다
go out [gou aut] 나가다, 외출하다
last year [last 'jiər] 지난해, 작년
middle school ['midl sku:l] 중학교
over and over again ['ouvər ænd 'ouvər ə'gen] 몇 번이고 반복해서
since then [sins ðen] 그때부터
sit on [sit ɔ:n] ~위에 앉다
start to ~하기 시작하다
walk along the street 길을 걷다, 길을 따라서 걷다

⑤ 과거완료 진행 (had been ~ing)
먼 과거부터 그 이후의 어떤 과거까지 계속되었음을 강조할 때 사용한다.

He had been sitting on the chair for five hours.
그는 다섯 시간 동안 계속 의자에 앉아있었다.

Then his back started to hurt.
그러자 허리가 아파왔다. (아파오기 시작했다.)

But he decided to study English again a month ago.
그러나 그는 한 달 전에 다시 영어 공부를 하기로 결심했다.

종합 이해

I had studied English for ten years since middle school. But I had never understood English well. I had never spoken English fluently. I had never read English well. I had never written English well. But I had received good grades on English tests.

After university I didn't study English at all. I decided to study English three years ago. I started to study English again. I studied English really hard every day. But I could not speak English fluently.

I started to study English three years ago. I have been studying English for three years. But I have never understood English well. I have been studying English for three years. But I have never spoken English fluently. I have been studying English for three years. But I have never read English well. And I have never written English well, either.

I have recently found the best way to master English. So I study harder to master English. I study English every day. I listen to English every day. I read English every day. I write English every day.

Now I am studying English in the library. I am reading an English book in the library. I am listening to English. I am writing an English essay in the library.

I am going to study in the library until late at night. I will study hard until I can understand English well. I will study hard until I can speak English fluently. I will study hard until I can read English well. Now I know the best way to master English. So I don't think it will take a long time to master English.

단어 및 숙어

best : good [gud] < better [ˈbetər] < best [best] 최고의, 가장 좋은
decide [diˈsaid] 결정하다, 결심하다
either [ˈiːðər] 각각 / ～도
essay [ˈesei] (학교의) 작문 숙제, 에세이
find [faind] / found [faund] / found [faund] 발견하다
fluently [ˈfluːəntli] 술술, 유창하게
grade [greid] 성적, 등급
harder [ˈhardər] 더 열심히
late [leit] 늦은, 지각한
library [ˈlaibreri] 도서관
listen [ˈlisn] 듣다, 경청하다
master [ˈmæstər] 통달하다, 마스터 하다
never [ˈnevər] 결코 ～이 아니다
read [riːd] / read [red] / read [red] 읽다
receive [riˈsiːv] 받다
recently [ˈriːsntli] 최근에
since [sins] ～이후로
speak [spiːk] / spoke [spouk] / spoken [spoukn] 이야기하다
start [staːrt] 시작하다, 출발하다
understand [ʌndərˈstænd] / understood [ʌndərˈstud] / understood [ʌndərˈstud] 이해하다
university [juːniˈvəːrsəti] 대학교, 종합대학
until [ənˈtil] ～할 때까지, –까지
write [rait] / wrote [rout] / written [writn] 쓰다, 작문하다

decide to ～하기로 결심하다, ～하기로 결정하다
English tests 영어 시험
for ten years 10년 동안
for three years 3년 동안
had never spoken fluently 결코 유창하게 말해본 적이 없었다
had never understood well 결코 잘 이해해본 적이 없었다
have been studying 쭉 공부를 해왔었다
have never read well 결코 잘 읽어 본 적이 없다
have never spoken fluently 결코 유창하게 말해본 적이 없다
have recently found 최근에 발견하였다
in the library 도서관에서
listen to 주의 깊게 듣다, 경청하다
not～ at all 전혀 ～이 아니다.
receive a good grade 좋은 성적을 받다 / receive good grades 좋은 성적들을 받다
start to ～하기 시작하다
the best way to master English 영어를 마스터하는 최고의 방법
until late at night 밤늦게까지

해설

I had studied English for ten years since middle school.
나는 중학교 이후로 10년 동안 영어 공부를 해왔었다.

But I had received good grades on English tests.
그러나 영어 시험에서는 좋은 점수를 받았다.

After university I didn't study English at all.
대학을 졸업한 후로 나는 영어 공부를 전혀 하지 않았다.

I have been studying English for three years.
나는 3년 동안 영어 공부를 쭉 해왔었다.

I have recently found the best way to master English.
나는 최근에 영어를 마스터하는 최고의 방법을 찾았다.

So I don't think it will take a long time to master English.
그래서 영어를 마스터하는 데 오랜 시간이 걸릴 것이라고는 생각하지 않는다.

PART 04.
부정문
의문문
명령문

01 부정문 ① be 동사가 있는 문장

I am an adult and I am not a child.
I am a prince and I'm not a princess.
You are a princess and you are not a prince.
You're a lady and you aren't a girl.
He is a king and he is not a queen.
She's a queen and she isn't a king.
It is a lion and it isn't a tiger.
It's is a tiger and it isn't a lion.
They are princesses and they aren't queens.
They're lions and they aren't tigers.

01 부정문 ② 일반 동사

I like the prince but I do not like the princess.
You like the princess but you don't like the prince.
He hates the king but he does not hate the queen.
She hates the queen but she doesn't hate the king.
A lion eats meat but it doesn't eat plants. That means it only eat meat.
The rabbits eat plants. The rabbits don't eat meat. That means they only eat plants.

단어 및 숙어

adult[əˈdʌlt] 성인, 어른
animal [ˈænɪməl] 동물, 짐승
eat [i:t] 먹다, 식사하다
hate [heit] 싫어하다, 미워하다
lion [ˈlaiən] 사자, 용맹스러운 사나이
mean [mi:n] 의미하다
meat [mi:t] 고기
only [ˈounli] 오직, 유일한
plant [plænt] 식물
prince [prins] 왕자
princess [ˈprinses] 공주
queen [kwi:n] 여왕, 왕비
rabbit [ˈræbit] 토끼
tiger [ˈtaigər] 호랑이

That means [ðæt mi:nz]
그것은 ~을 의미한다

01 부정문 ③ 조동사

I can run but I can not run fast.
I can swim in the river but I can't fly in the sky.
A bird can fly in the sky but it can't swim in the river.
I will leave my house and I will not come back to my house.

02 의문문 ① be 동사가 있는 문장

"Am I ugly?" "No, you are not. You are beautiful."
"Are you a queen?" "No, I am not. I am a princess."
"Are you a nurse and are you Mary?" "No, I'm not. I'm not a nurse. And I'm Jane"
"Is he a king?" "No, he is not. He is a prince."
"Is she a queen?" "No, she isn't. She's a princess."
"Is it a lion?" "No, it isn't. It's a tiger."
"Are they birds?" "No, they are not. They are bees."
"Are they bees?" "No, they aren't. They're birds."

02 의문문 ② 일반 동사

"Do you like dogs" "Yes, I do. I like dogs very much."
"Do you like cats" "No, I don't. I like dogs very much."
"Take a guess! Do I like cows?" "Yes, you do. You like cows."
"Take a guess! Do I like horses?" " No, you don't. I know you don't like horses. You like cows."

단어 및 숙어

aren't [arnt] are not의 줄임말
bee [bi:] 벌, 일꾼
bird [bə:rd] 새
can't [kænt] can not의 줄임말
cat [kæt] 고양이
cow [kau] 소(동물)
don't [dount] do not의 줄임말
fly [flai] 비행하다, 날다
guess [ges] 추측하다, 알아맞히다
horse [hɔ:rs] 말
I'm [aim] I am의 줄임말
isn't [iznt] is not의 줄임말
It's It is의 줄임말
leave [li:v] 떠나다
lion ['laiən] 사자
prince [prins] 왕자
princess ['prinses] 공주

queen [kwi:n] 여왕, 왕비
river ['rivər] 강
She's she is의 줄임말
sky [skai] 하늘, 천국
swim [swim] 수영하다, 헤엄치다
tiger ['taigər] 호랑이
ugly ['ʌgli] 못생긴, 비열한

come back to [kʌm bæk tu:]
~로 돌아오다
fly in the sky [flai in ðə skai]
하늘을 날다
in the river [in ðə 'rivər] 강에서
in the sky [in ðə skai] 하늘에서

해설

의문문

be 동사나 can, will 등 조동사가 있는 문장은 be 동사나 조동사를 문장의 맨 앞에 두어 의문문을 만든다. be 동사나 조동사가 없는 문장은 do 동사를 문장의 맨 앞에 두어 의문문을 만든다.

I will leave my house and I will not come back to my house.
집을 떠나서 돌아오지 않을 것이다.

Are you a nurse and are you Mary?
당신은 간호사이고 (이름이) 메리입니까?

Take a guess!
맞혀봐!

"Does he like horses?" "Yes, he does. He likes horses."
"Does she like horses?" "No, she doesn't. She likes cows."
"Do the bees like honey?" "Yes, they do. They like honey."

02 의문문 ③ 조동사(can will be going to...)

"Can you swim?" "Yes, I can. I can swim in the river."
"Can you fly in the sky?" "No, I can't. But I can swim in the river."
"Can he run fast?" "No, he can't. But he can walk fast."

"Will you go to church tomorrow?" "Yes, I will go to church tomorrow."
"Will you go to the park tomorrow?" "Yes, I'll go to the park tomorrow."
"Will you go to the park tomorrow?" "No, I won't. I'll go to church tomorrow."

"Are you going to do your homework?" "Yes, I am going to do my homework."
"Are you going to go to bed early tonight?" "No. I'm not. I'm going to go to bed late tonight."

단어 및 숙어

bee [biː] 벌
can't [kænt] can not의 줄임말
church [tʃəːrtʃ] 교회, 예배당
cow [kau] 소
doesn't [ˈdʌznt] does not의 줄임말
fly [flai] 비행하다, 날다
homework [ˈhoumwəːrk] 숙제, 가정에서 하는 일
honey [ˈhʌni] 꿀, 벌꿀
horse [hɔːrs] 말
horses [hɔːrsiz] (horse의 복수) 말들
I'll [ail] I will의 줄임말
late [leit] 늦은
park [paːrk] 공원
river [ˈrivər] 강
sky [skai] 하늘, 천국
swim [swim] 수영하다, 헤엄치다
tomorrow [tuˈmarou] 내일
tonight [tuˈnait] 오늘밤
won't [wount] will not의 줄임말

be going to ~할 예정이다.
go to bed 자다, 잠자리에 들다

02 의문문 ④ 의문사 (who, what...)가 있는 의문문

A : I am a doctor. Who are you?
B : I am a nurse and my name is Mary.
A : Are you a nurse and are you Mary?
B : Yes, I am.

A : I am in the room. Where are you?
B : I am here. I am in the kitchen.
A : Are you in the kitchen?
B : Yes, I am.

A : What are you going to do tomorrow?
B : I am going to clean my house tomorrow.
A : Are you going to clean your house tomorrow?
B : Yes, I'm going to clean my house tomorrow.

A : You look tired. Why do you look so tired?
B : I slept late last night.
A : Why did you slept late?
B : Don't ask. It's my privacy.

단어 및 숙어

clean [kli:n] 청소하다 / 깨끗한
doctor [ˈdɑ:ktər] 의사, 박사
here [hiər] 여기
kitchen [ˈkitʃin] 부엌, 주방
late [leit] 늦은, 늦게
look [luk] 보다, 보인다
Mary [meəri] 여자 이름
nurse [nə:rs] 간호사
privacy [ˈpraivəsi] 프라이버시, 사생활
sleep [sli:p] / slept [slept] /
slept [slept] 잠자다
tired [taiərd] 피곤한

be going to ~할 예정이다

02 의문문 ⑤ 부가 의문문

A : You are a teacher, aren't you?
B : Yes, I am.
A : You aren't tired, are you?
B : Yes, I am tired.

A : You go to church, don't you?
B : Yes, I do. I go to church every sunday.
A : You don't like sports, do you?
B : Yes, I do. I like sports very much.

A : Your brother isn't tall, is he?
B : No, he isn't. He is short.
A : Your sister isn't fat, is she?
B : Yes, she is. She is really fat.

03 명령문

I ran and shouted in the room last night. So my mom said, "It's too loud. Be quiet!"

The window is open. It's too cold. Close the window, please. And don't open the window again.

단어 및 숙어

church [tʃəːrtʃ] 교회
close [klouz] (문 등을)닫다
cold [kould] 추운, 차가운
fat [fæt] 살찐
loud [laud] 시끄러운
open [ˈoupn] 열려있는, 열다
quiet [kwaiət] 조용한
run [rʌn] / ran [ræn] / run [rʌn] 달리다

short [ʃɔːrt] 키가 작은, 짧은
shout [ʃaut] 외치다, 고함치다
Sunday [ˈsʌndei] 일요일
tall [tɔːl] 키가 큰
window [ˈwindou] 창문
tired [taiərd] 피곤한

be going to ~할 예정이다

해설

⑤ **부가 의문문** : 일반 문장의 끝에 동사와 주어를 덧붙여 의문문을 만든다.
앞 문장이 긍정문이면 부정을 덧붙이고 앞 문장이 부정문이면 긍정을 덧붙여 의문문을 만든다.

You go to church, don't you? : 너는 교회에 간다. 그렇지? (너는 교회에 가는 거지 그렇지?)

질문에 대답을 할 때 상대방이 묻는 질문의 내용과 상관없이 자신의 대답이 긍정문이면 Yes로 대답하고 자신의 대답이 부정문이면 No로 대답한다.

A : Your brother isn't tall, is he? 너의 형은 키가 크지 않지 그렇지?
B : No, he isn't. He is short. 응 크지 않아. 형은 작아.

A : You aren't tired, are you? 너는 피곤하지 않지 그렇지?
B : Yes, I am tired. 아니, 나는 피곤해.

A : Your sister isn't fat, is she? 너의 언니는 뚱뚱하지 않지 그렇지?
B : Yes, she is. She is really fat. 아니야 뚱뚱해. 언니는 진짜 뚱뚱해.

명령문 : 명령문에서는 일반적으로 주어를 생략한다.

It's too loud. Be quiet! 너무 시끄럽구나. 조용히 해라.

Close the window, please. And don't open the window again.
창문 좀 닫아주세요. 그리고 창문을 다시 열지 말아 주세요.

04 명령문, and ~ 명령문, or~

Finish your homework, and I will give you money.
Be kind to people, and you can make many friends.

Finish your job, or I will not give you money.
Be quiet, or I will give you lots of homework.

Study hard, and you will receive a good grade. And do your homework everyday, or you will receive a bad grade.

단어 및 숙어

finish [ˈfiniʃ] 끝나다, 끝내다
grade [greid] 성적, 등급
job [dʒa:b] 할 일, 직업
kind [kaind] 친절한 / 종류
quiet [kwaiət] 조용한

receive a bad grade
[get ə bæd greid] 나쁜 성적을 받다
receive a good grade
[get ə gud greid] 좋은 성적을 받다
lots of [la:ts əv] 많은
make friends [meik frendz]
친구를 사귀다(친구를 만들다)

해설

명령문, and ~ : ~해라 그러면 ~할 것이다.

Be kind to people, and you can make a lot of friends.
사람들에게 친절하게 대하여라. 그러면 많은 친구를 사귈 수 있다.

명령문, or~ : ~해라 그렇지 않으면 ~할 것이다.

Be quiet, or I will give you lots of homework.
조용히 해라. 안 그러면 숙제를 많이 내줄 테다.

Study hard, and you will receive a good grade.
열심히 공부해라 그러면 좋은 성적을 받을 것이다.

And do your homework everyday, or you will receive a bad grade.
그리고 매일 숙제를 해라 그렇지 않으면 나쁜 성적을 받을 것이다.

PART 05.
비교

01 비교급 ① (~er than)

I'm older than Tom. I'm stronger than Tom. I am heavier than him. I'm taller than him. I can run faster than him. But he is smarter than me. His grade is better than mine. He knows better than me. He is kinder than me. I think he is much nicer than me.

Mary is beautiful. Jane is beautiful, too. But Mary is more beautiful than Jane.

This book is interesting. That book is interesting, too. But this book is more interesting than that book.

01 비교급 ② The + 비교급, The + 비교급

We need your help. The sooner, the better. The more, the better. The more you know us, the more you can help us.

단어 및 숙어

better [ˈbetər]
더 나은, 더 잘 ~한(good, well의 비교급)
well 잘
[wel] < better [ˈbetər] < best [best],
good 좋은
[gud] < better [ˈbetər] < best [best]
grade [greid] 성적, 등급
heavy [ˈhevi] 무거운
interesting [ˈintərestiŋ]
흥미 있는, 재미있는
Jane [dʒein] 제인(여자 이름)
kind [kaind] 친절한 / 종류
Mary [meəri] 메리(여자 이름)
mine [main] 내 것, 나의 것

more [mɔːr] 더(더 많은 더 좋은,
much, a lot of, many의 비교급)
much [mʌtʃ] < more [mɔːr]
 < most [moust]
many [ˈmeni] < more [mɔːr]
 < most [moust]
need [niːd] 필요로 하다
old [ould] 나이가 많은, 늙은
smart [smaːrt] 똑똑한, 깔끔한
sooner [ˈsuːnər] soon(곧)의 비교급
strong [strɔːŋ] 강한, 힘이 센
tall [tɔːl] 키가 큰, 높은
than [ðæn] ~보다

해설

비교급

① (~er than)

I'm older than Tom. 나는 Tom 보다 나이가 많다.
He knows better than me. 그는 나보다 더 잘 안다. (아는 것이 많다.)
I think he is much nicer than me. 그는 나보다 훨씬 멋있다.
Mary is more beautiful than Jane. 메리는 제인보다 더 아름답다.

* –ful, – able 등으로 끝나는 형용사나 3음절 이상의 형용사는 more, most를 사용하여 비교급과 최상급을 만든다.

② **The + 비교급, The + 비교급 : ~할수록 더 ~하다.**
The sooner, the better. The more, the better. The more you know us, the more you can help us.
빠를수록 더 좋다. 더 많을수록 더 좋다. 우리에 대해서 더 많이 알수록 우리를 더 도울 수 있다.

02 최상급 (the + -(e)st)

Tom is a smart student. Tom is the smartest student in the class.
Seoul is a big city. Seoul is the biggest city in Korea. And Seoul is one of the biggest cities in the world.

Jane is smart. Jane is beautiful. Jane is the smartest student in the class. And Jane is the most beautiful student in the class.

03 의미상 최상급 (비교급 + than any other 단수 명사)

Mary is beautiful. She is very beautiful. She is more beautiful than any other girl in the class.

Tom is strong. He is very strong. He is stronger than any other boy in the class.

Dick is tall. He is very tall. He is taller than any other student in the class.

단어 및 숙어

any [ˈeni] 어떤
city [ˈsiti] 도시
class [klæs] 학급, 반
Dick [dik] 딕(남자 이름)
Jane [dʒein] 제인(여자 이름)
Korea [Kɔːˈriə]
한국(악센트 주의 2음절에 악센트가 있음)
most [moust] 가장 ~한, 가장 많은
(a lot of, many, much의 최상급)
a lot of [ə lat ʌv] < more [mɔːr]
< most [moust],
many [ˈmeni] < more [mɔːr]
< most [moust]
much [mʌtʃ] < more [mɔːr]
< most [moust]

other [ˈʌðər] 다른, 다른 사람
Seoul [soul] 서울
smart [smaːrt] 똑똑한, 깔끔한
strong [strɔːŋ] 강한, 힘이 센
tall [tɔːl] 키가 큰, 높은
world [wəːrld] 세계, 세상

in the class [in ðə klæs]
반에서, 학급에서
in the world [in ðə wərld]
이 세상에, 세계에서
one of [wʌn əv] ~ 중의 하나

해설

최상급 (the + −(e)st) : 가장 ~한

Seoul is the biggest city in Korea. And Seoul is one of the biggest cities in the world.
서울은 한국에서 가장 큰 도시이다. 그리고 서울은 세계에서 가장 큰 도시 중 하나이다.

비교급 + than any other 단수 명사

최상급의 의미 : 무엇보다 더 ~하다 → 가장 ~하다
She is more beautiful than any other girl in the class.
그녀는 학급에서 그 누구보다 아름다운 소녀이다. (가장 아름답다.)

시험 연구

학교 시험이나 토익에서 비교급 + than any other 다음에 오는 명사 형태를 묻는 문제가 자주 출제된다.
: 위 문장에서 more beautiful than any other girl (O) more beautiful than any other girls (X)

PART 06.
수동태

01 현재 시제 ① 능동형 문장

It is sunday. I get up late. I open the window. Mom prepares a meal. When I have brunch, I break the dishes. After brunch I read a book. And I write a letter. And then I clean my room.

01 현재 시제 ② 수동형 문장 (be 동사 현재형 + 과거분사)

It is sunday. I get up late. The window is opened by me. A meal is prepared by my mom. When I have brunch, the dishes are broken by me. After brunch a book is read by me. And a letter is written by me. And then my room is cleaned by me.

02 현재 진행형 ① 능동형 문장

I am opening the window. Mom is preparing a meal. I am breaking the dishes. I am reading a book. I am writing a letter. I am cleaning my room.

단어 및 숙어

break [breik] 깨다, 깨지다
broken ['broukn]
break의 과거분사 break
[breik] / broke[brouk] /
broken [broukn]
brunch [brʌntʃ] 늦은 아침 식사, 아점
by [bai] ~에 의한, 옆
dish [diʃ] 음식, 접시
late [leit] 늦은 늦게
meal [mi:l] 식사, 한 끼
prepare [pri'peər] 준비하다, 준비시키다
read [red] read의 과거분사
read [ri:d] / read [red] / read [red]
some [sʌm] 몇 개의 조금의
sunday ['sʌndei] 일요일
window ['windou] 창문
written [ritn] write의 과거분사
write [rait] / wrote / [rout] /
written [ritn]

and then [ænd ðen] 그리고 나서
break the dishes [breik ðə diʃiz]
접시를 깨뜨리다
get up [get ʌp] (잠자리 등에서)일어나다
have brunch [hæv brʌntʃ]
아점을 먹다, 늦은 아침을 먹다
prepare a meal [pri'peər ə mi:l]
식사를 준비하다
read a book [ri:d ə buk]
책을 읽다, 독서하다
write a letter [rait ə 'letər]
편지를 쓰다

해설

수동태

어떤 동작이나 상태가 수동적으로 이루어짐을 강조할 때 사용한다.
by + 행위자는 생략되는 경우가 많다.

현재 시제의 수동형 (be 동사 현재 + 과거분사 + by 목적격)

The window is opened by me. A meal is prepared by my mom.
창문은 나에 의해서 열린다. 식사가 엄마에 의해서 준비된다.

02 현재 진행형
② 수동형 문장 (be 동사 현재형 + being + 과거분사)

The window is being opened by me. A meal is being prepared by mom. The dishes are being broken by me. A book is being read by me. A letter is being written by me. My room is being cleaned by me.

03 과거 시제 ① 능동형 문장

It was sunday. I got up late. I opened the window. Mom prepared a meal. When I had brunch, I broke the dishes. After brunch I read a book. And I wrote a letter. And then I cleaned my room.

03 과거 시제 ② 수동형 문장 (be 동사의 과거형 + 과거분사)

It was sunday. I got up late. The window was opened by me. A meal was prepared by my mom. When I had brunch, the dishes were broken by me. After brunch a book was read by me. And a letter was written by me. And then my room was cleaned by me.

단어 및 숙어

break [breik] 깨다, 깨지다
broken ['broukn] break의 과거분사
break [breik] / broke [brouk] / broken [broukn]
brunch [brʌntʃ] 늦은 아침 식사, 아점
by [bai] ~에 의한, 옆
dish [diʃ] 음식, 접시
late [leit] 늦은 늦게
meal [mi:l] 식사, 한 끼
prepare [pri'peər] 준비하다, 준비시키다
read [ri:d] / read [red] / read [red]
some [sʌm] 몇 개의 조금의
sunday ['sʌndei] 일요일
window ['windou] 창문
written [ritn] write의 과거분사
write [rait] / wrote / [rout] / written [ritn]

and then [ænd ðen] 그리고 나서
break the dishes [breik ðə diʃiz]
접시를 깨뜨리다
get up [get ʌp] (잠자리 등에서)일어나다
have brunch [hæv brʌntʃ]
아점을 먹다, 늦은 아침을 먹다
prepare a meal [pri'peər ə mi:l]
식사를 준비하다
read a book [ri:d ə buk]
책을 읽다, 독서하다
write a letter [rait ə 'letər]
편지를 쓰다

해설

현재 진행형의 수동태
(be 동사 현재형 + being + 과거분사)

The window is being opened by me. A meal is being prepared by mom.
창문이 나에 의해서 열리고 있다. 식사가 엄마에 의해서 준비되고 있다.

과거 시제의 수동형
(be 동사의 과거 + 과거분사+ by 행위자)

The window was opened by me. A meal was prepared by my mom.
창문이 나에 의해서 열렸다. 식사가 엄마에 의해서 준비되었다.

04 현재완료 시제 ① 능동형

It was sunday. I got up late. And I have opened the window. Mom has prepared a meal. I have broken the dishes. I have read some books. I have written some letters. I have cleaned my room.

04 현재완료 시제 ② 수동형 (have been + 과거분사)

It was sunday. I got up late. The window has been opened by me. A meal has been prepared by mom. The dishes have been broken by me. Some books have been read by me. Some letters have been written by me. My room has been cleaned by me.

05 미래 시제 ① 능동형 문장

I will get up late tomorrow. After getting up, I will open the window. Mom will prepare a meal tomorrow morning. After breakfast I will write a letter. And then I will clean my room.

05 미래 시제 ② 수동형 문장 (will be + 과거분사)

I will get up late tomorrow. The window will be opened by me. A meal will be prepared by my mom. And a letter will be written by me. And then my room will be cleaned by me.

단어 및 숙어

break [breik] 깨다, 깨지다
broken [ˈbroukn] break의 과거분사
break [breik] / broke [brouk] / broken [broukn]
brunch [brʌntʃ] 늦은 아침 식사, 아점
by [bai] ~에 의한, 옆
dish [diʃ] 음식, 접시
late [leit] 늦은 늦게
meal [mi:l] 식사, 한 끼
prepare [priˈpeər] 준비하다, 준비시키다
read [red] read의 과거분사
read [ri:d] / read [red] / read [red]
some [sʌm] 몇 개의 조금의
sunday [ˈsʌndei] 일요일
window [ˈwindou] 창문
written [ritn] write의 과거분사
write [rait] / wrote / [rout] / written [ritn]

and then [ænd ðen] 그리고 나서
break the dishes [breik ðə diʃiz]
접시를 깨뜨리다
get up [get ʌp] (잠자리 등에서)일어나다
have brunch [hæv brʌntʃ]
아점을 먹다, 늦은 아침을 먹다
prepare a meal [priˈpeər ə mi:l]
식사를 준비하다
read a book [ri:d ə buk]
책을 읽다, 독서하다
write a letter [rait ə ˈletər]
편지를 쓰다

해설

현재완료 수동형
(have been + 과거분사)

The window has been opened by me. A meal has been prepared by mom.
창문이 나에 의해서 열렸었다. 식사는 엄마에 의해서 준비되었었다.

미래 시제의 수동형
(will be + 과거분사+ by 행위자)

The window will be opened by me. 창문이 나에 의해서 열릴 것이다.
A meal will be prepared by my mom. 식사가 엄마에 의해서 준비될 것이다.

PART 07.
동명사

01 주어 역할

Getting up early is good. And going to school early is good, too. Getting up late is bad. Going to school late is not good, either.

Going to bed early is good. I mean, sleeping early is good. Going to bed late is bad. I mean, sleeping late is not good.

I think going to bed early and getting up early is a good habit.
I think going to bed late and getting up late is a bad habit.

02 보어 역할

The teacher's job is teaching. My English teacher's job is teaching English. My job is learning. My job is learning English and studying English.

My hobby is playing soccer. My dream is traveling in Europe. But my real dream is becoming a doctor. So my job is studying hard. Jane's hobby is playing the piano. Her dream is becoming a pianist. So her job is playing the piano well.

단어 및 숙어

hobby [ˈhaːbi] 취미
Jane [ˈdʒein] 여자 이름
job [dʒaːb] 할 일, 직업
learn [lərn] 배우다
mean [miːn] 의미하다
pianist [ˈpiːənist] 피아니스트
sleep [sliːp] 잠자다
soccer [ˈsaːkər] 축구
travel [ˈtrævəl] 여행하다

Jane's hobby 제인의 취미
(명사에 's를 붙여서 소유격을 만듬)
not~ either [naːt ˈiːðər]
~ 또한 ~가 아니다
play soccer 축구를 하다
play the piano 피아노를 치다
teacher's job 선생님의 할 일
(명사에 's를 붙여서 소유격을 만듬)
travel in ~를 여행하다.
I mean [ai miːn] 무슨 말인가 하면, 다시 말해서(자신이 한 말을 다시 설명하거나 수정할 때 씀)

해설

동명사 : 동사의 원형에 ing를 붙여서 명사의 역할(주어, 목적어, 보어 역할)을 하게 한다.

주어 역할

Getting up early is good. And Going to school early is good, too.
(Getting up → 일어나는 것, Going → 가는 것)
일찍 일어나는 것은 좋다. 학교에 일찍 가는 것도 역시 좋다.

참고) I think going to bed early and getting up early is a good habit.
A and B 는 일반적으로 복수 취급하기 때문에 위의 문장에서 are가 쓰일 수도 있으나 '일찍 자고 일찍 일어나는 것'을 하나의 사건으로 보고 단수 취급하여 is가 쓰였다.

보어 역할

The teacher's job is teaching. My English teacher's job is teaching English.
선생님의 할 일은 가르치는 것이다. 나의 영어 선생님의 할 일은 영어를 가르치는 것이다.

03 목적어 역할

Tom enjoys swimming. Jane enjoys swimming, too. They all enjoy swimming. They enjoy swimming in the pool. But they do not enjoy swimming in the river.

My father enjoyed smoking. My mother enjoyed smoking, too. My father still enjoys smoking. But my mother quit smoking. She does not smoke any more. I think my father will not quit smoking. He really enjoys smoking.

I didn't mind fighting. I enjoyed fighting. But I gave up fighting. Because I am not a kid any more. Now my job is studying hard.

A : Would you mind opening the door?
B : I'm sorry. I do
A : What? What did you say?
B : I mean I mind opening the door. Because it's too cold.
A : Okay I see. I will go outside.

단어 및 숙어

enjoy [inˈdʒɔi] 즐기다
fight [fait] 싸우다
give [giv] / gave [geiv] / given [givn] 주다
give up [giv ʌp] 포기하다, 그만두다
kid [kid] 아이
mind [maind]
~을 꺼리다, 언짢아하다 / 마음, 정신
pool [pu:l] 수영장
quit [kwit] 그만두다, 그만하다
river [ˈrivər] 강
smoke [smouk] 담배를 피우다, 연기

swim [swim] 수영하다

go outside 나가다 외출하다
I see 알겠다, 그렇군요
in the pool 수영장에서
in the river 강에서
not ~ any more
이젠 ~이 아니다 / 더 이상 ~이 아니다
Would you mind ~ing
~해도 괜찮겠습니까?
(~하는 것이 싫으십니까?)

해설

목적어 역할

Tom enjoys swimming. Jane enjoys swimming, too.
톰은 수영하는 것을 즐긴다. 제인도 역시 수영하는 것을 즐긴다.

I didn't mind fighting. I enjoyed fighting.
나는 싸우는 것을 마다하지 (꺼리지) 않았다. 나는 싸우는 것을 즐겼다.

Would you mind opening the window? I'm sorry. I do
당신은 창문을 여는 것을 꺼리시나요? → 창문 좀 열어도 되겠습니까?
미안한데요. 나는 싫습니다. → 여기서 do는 mind(싫다, 꺼린다)의 의미

시험 연구

목적어로 부정사만을 취하는가 동명사만을 취하는가를 묻는 문제는 토익, 수능, 학교 시험에서 단골로 출제됩니다. 수험생이 아닌 학습자님들은 아랫부분은 굳이 볼 필요가 없습니다. 운전면허 필기시험을 잘 본다고 운전을 잘하는 것은 아니잖아요.

부정사를 목적어로 취하지 않고 동명사만을 목적어로 취하는 동사
quit avoid, mind, enjoy, finish, give up, admit, deny, escape, consider, postpone, put off, resist 암기 요령 : **크!**(quit) **여보**(avoid) **미**(mind) **엔~**(enjoy), **피**(finish)나잖아 포**기**(give up)해! **어**(admit) **데**(deny)**에서**(escape) **콘**(consider) **포스트**(postpone) **푸**(put off)**레**(resist)요

중학생은 **크!**(quit) **여보**(avoid) **미**(mind) **엔~**(enjoy), **피**(finish)나잖아 포**기**(give up)해! 정도만 외워도 될 것입니다.

종합 이해

My hobby is swimming. I enjoy swimming. I don't mind swimming in the river. But swimming in the river is dangerous. So I don't enjoy swimming in the river. I enjoy swimming in the pool instead.

I don't mind working on the weekends. Working on the weekends is not so hard to me. And I have a large family. So making a lot of money is important to me. But sometimes I need a break. So I stopped working on the weekends. But I didn't give up making money. I just need a break for a while.

I take a walk. I usually take a walk after dinner. Taking a walk after dinner is good for my health. And I usually exercise after taking a walk. And I usually take a shower after exercise.

I like taking a shower. Taking a shower after exercise is really good. Think about taking a shower after exercising on a hot day.

단어 및 숙어

break [breik] 휴식 / 깨뜨리다
dangerous [ˈdeindʒərəs] 위험한
dinner [ˈdinər] 저녁 식사
exercise [ˈeksərsaiz] 운동, 운동하다
health [helθ] 건강
hobby [ˈhaːbi] 취미
hot [haːt] 더운, 뜨거운
important [imˈpɔːrtənt] 중요한
instead [inˈsted] 대신에
just [dʒʌst] 단지, 정확히
mind [maind] 싫어하다, 꺼리다
need [niːd] ~을 필요로 하다
shower [ʃauər] 샤워, 소나기
sometimes [ˈsʌmtaimz] 가끔
usually [ˈjuːʒuəli] 보통 대개
walk [wɔːk] 걷다
weekend [wiːkend] 주말
while [wail] ~하는 동안에

a large family [ə laːrdʒ ˈfæməli]
대가족
for a while [fɔːr ə wail]
잠깐, 얼마동안
give up [giv ʌp] 포기하다
have a large family
[hæv ə laːrdʒ ˈfæməli] 식구가 많다.
in the pool [in ðə puːl] 풀장에서
in the river [in ðə ˈrivər] 강에서
make money [meik ˈmʌni] 돈을 벌다
on a hot day [ɔːn ə haːt dei]
더운 날에
on the weekend [ɔːn ðə ˈwiːkend]
주말에
take a shower [teik ə ʃauər]
샤워하다
take a walk [teik ə wɔːk] 산책하다
think about [θiŋk əˈbaut]
~에 대해 생각하다

해설

I don't mind swimming in the river.
강에서 수영하는 것(swimming in the river)을 싫어하지는 않는다.

But swimming in the river is dangerous. 강에서 수영하는 것은 위험하다.
주어

I enjoy swimming in the pool instead.
대신에 수영장에서 수영하는 것을 즐긴다.

Working on the weekends is not so hard to me.
주말에 일하는 것(Working on the weekends)은 나에게(to me) 그렇게 힘들지 않다.(not so hard)

I have a large family.
식구가 많다.

So making much money is important to me.
돈을 많이 버는 것(making a lot of money)은 나에게 중요하다.

I just need a break for a while.
나는 단지 잠시 휴식이 필요할 뿐이다.

Taking a walk after dinner is good for my health.
저녁 식사 후에 산책을 하는 것(Taking a walk after dinner)은 건강에 좋다.

Taking a shower after exercise is really good.
운동 후에 샤워하는 것(Taking a shower after exercise)은 정말 좋다.

Think about (taking a shower after exercising on a hot day.)
더운 날에 운동을 한 후에 샤워하는 것(taking a shower after exercising on a hot day.)을 생각해 보아라.

PART 08.
부정사

01 명사 역할 ① 일반 형태

(01)

To learn is hard. But to teach is hard, too.

(02)

To see is to believe. To see something is to believe it. To experience is to believe. To experience something is to believe it. To understand something is to know it. To know more about the world and life is to become a better person.

(03)

To know myself was very difficult. To understand life was very difficult, too. When I was a kid, I wanted to know lots of things. I wanted to learn a lot of things. I wanted to learn how to swim. I wanted to know how to study well. I wanted to learn how to play baseball. I wanted to know how to be famous. I wanted to know……

They gave me the answers. They taught me a lot of things. But what I really wanted to know is something different. But they could not give me the answer to it.

단어 및 숙어

answer [ˈænsər] 대답, 대답하다
baseball [ˈbeisbɔ:l] 야구
believe [biˈli:v] 믿다
good [gud] < better [ˈbetər] < best [best]
can [kæn] / could [kud] / could [kud]
different [ˈdifərənt] 다른
difficult [ˈdifikəlt] 어려운
experience [ikˈspiəriəns] 경험, 경험하다
famous [ˈfeiməs] 유명한
hard [ha:rd] 어려운, 열심히
kid [kid] 아이
know [nou] 알다
learn [lərn] 배우다
myself [maiˈself] 내 자신
person [ˈpərsn] 사람
something [ˈsʌmθiŋ] 어떤 것
teach [ti:tʃ] / taught [tɔ:t] / taught [tɔ:t]
thing [θiŋ] (어떤) 것, 사물
understand [ʌndərˈstænd] 이해하다
want [wɔ:nt] 원하다

a better person [ə ˈbetər ˈpərsn] 더 나은 사람
a lot of = lots of 많은
how to + 동사 ~하는 법
how to be famous [hau tu: bi: ˈfeiməs] 유명해지는 법
how to swim [hau tu: swim] 수영하는 법
the world and life [ðə wərld ænd laif] 세상과 인생
want to [wɔ:nt tu:] ~하기를 원하다
play baseball 야구를 하다

해설

To learn is hard. But to teach is hard, too.
배우는 것은 어렵다. 그러나 가르치는 것도 역시 어렵다.

To see is to believe.
보는 것이 믿는 것이다. → 보면 믿는다. → 백문이 불여일견이다.

To see something is to believe it.
무언가 본다는 것은 그것을 믿는 것이다. → 본 것은 믿는다.

To experience something is to believe it.
무엇을 경험하는 것은 그것을 믿는 것이다. → 경험한 것은 믿는다.

To know more about the world and life is to become a better person.
세상과 삶에 대해서 더 안다는 것은 더 나은 사람이 되는 것이다.

When I was a kid, I wanted to know lots of things.
어렸을 때 나는 많은 것을 알고 싶었다.

I wanted to learn how to swim.
나는 수영하는 법을 배우고 싶었다.

how to + 동사 : ~ 하는 법

how to study well.
공부를 잘하는 법

how to play baseball.
야구하는 법

I wanted to know how to be famous.
나는 유명해지는 법을 알고 싶었다.

They taught me a lot of things.
그들은 나에게 많은 것을 가르쳐 주었다.

what I really wanted to know is something different.
내가 정말로 알고 싶었던 것은 뭔가 다른 것이었다.

시험 연구
수험생이 아닌 분들은 볼 필요가 없습니다.

목적어로 부정사만을 취하는 동사(단골 출제)
expect, manage, promise, afford, hope, plan, decide, choose, desire, decide, want
[암기요령: **마!**(manage) **프로**(promise)가 **아파**(afford) **호~**(hope)하냐? **플랜**(plan) **데크**(decide)에서 **초**(choose)**대**(desire)를 **기대**(expect 기대하다)하고 **원**(want 원하다)하는데..]

01 명사 역할 ② 의문사 + to 부정사

I really wanted to know how to live. I wanted to become someone important. I wanted to become someone else. I wanted to go somewhere. I wanted to go somewhere nobody had gone before. But I did not know how to live. I did not know where to go. I did not know what to do. Nobody taught me how to live. Nobody taught me what to do. Nobody told me where to go.

01 명사 역할 ③ 기타 명사처럼 쓰이는 부정사

I wanted to go to the library. So I went to the library this morning.

I planned to go to the movies on a sunday. So I went to the movies last sunday.

I hoped to see her. So I went to her school. And I walked around the school.

단어 및 숙어

around [əˈraund] 주변에
else [els] 다른, 그 밖에
hope [houp] 희망, 희망하다.
important [imˈpɔːrtənt] 중요한
library [ˈlaibrəri] 도서관
movie [ˈmuːvi] 영화
nobody [ˈnoubaːdi] 아무도 ~않다
plan [plæn] 계획, 계획하다.
someone [ˈsʌmwʌn] 어떤 사람
somewhere [ˈsʌmweər]
어디론가, 어딘가에
Sunday [ˈsʌndei] 일요일
teach [tiːtʃ] / taught [tɔːt] /
taught [tɔːt] 가르치다
tell [tel] / told [tould] / told [tould]
말하다

want [wɔːnt] 원하다
go [gou] / went [went] /
gone [gɔːn]

go to the movies 영화 보러 가다
hope to ~하기를 희망하다
how to live 어떻게 살아야 할지, 사는 법
plan to ~할 계획이다
someone else 다른 어떤 사람
this morning 오늘 아침
walk around ~의 주변을 돌아다니다
want to ~을 원하다
what to do 무엇을 해야 할지, 할 일
where to go 어디로 가야 할지, 가야 할 곳

해설

how to + 동사 : ~하는 법
I really wanted to know how to live. 나는 어떻게 살아야 할지를 정말 알고 싶었다.
I wanted to go somewhere. 나는 어디론가 가고 싶었다.
I wanted to go somewhere nobody had been before.
나는 아무도 가보지 않은(nobody had been before.) 그 어딘가를 가고 싶었다.

where to go 어디를 가야 할지
what to do 무엇을 해야 할지
how to live 어떻게 살아야 할지

Nobody taught me what to do. : 아무도 무엇을 해야 할지 가르쳐 주지 않았다.
Nobody told me where to go. : 아무도 어디로 가야 할지 말해주지 않았다.

I hoped to see her. So I went to her school. And I walked around the school.
나는 그녀를 보고 싶었다. (희망했다.) 그래서 그녀의 학교로 가서 학교 주변을 배회했다.
(학교 주변을 걸으며 돌아 다녔다.)

02 형용사 역할

"Please help me. I have no family to help me. I have no relatives to help me. I have no friends to help me. There is no water to drink. Please give me some water to drink. I need food. Please give me something to eat. I need a friend to play with. Please be my friend. I need a lover to love. Please be my girlfriend. And I have no house to live in. Please, give me a house to live in. And I have no....."

"Who the hell are you?"
"I have no name. Please give me a name"
"You have an endless desire. So I name you 'Greed.'"

greed [griːd] 탐욕

"Thank you, sir. Please give me one more name."
"……,"

단어 및 숙어

desire [diˈzaiər] 욕망, 원하다
drink [driŋk] 마시다
eat [iːt] 먹다
endless [ˈendlis] 끝없는, 무한한
food [fuːd] 음식
greed [griːd] 탐욕
hell [hel] 지옥
help [help] 돕다
lover [ˈlʌvər] 연인

name [neim] ~라 이름을 짓다, 이름
need [niːd] 필요로 하다
relative [ˈrelətiv] 친척
sir [səːr] 선생님(존칭)
water [ˈwɔːtər] 물

live in ~에서 살다
one more 하나 더
play with ~와 놀다

해설

본문에서 밑줄을 그은 것은 전부 형용사 역할을 하는 것으로 한국어로 해석을 할 때는 주로 ~할, ~하는 등으로 해석하면 무난하다.

I have no family to help me. 나를 도와줄(to help me) 가족이 없습니다.
There is no water to drink. 마실(to drink) 물이 없습니다.
I have no house to live in. 살(to live in) 집이 없습니다.
I name you greed[griːd]. 탐욕이라고 이름을 지어주마.
Please give me one more name. 이름을 하나만 더 주세요.

Who the hell are you? 도대체 당신 누구요?
(상스런 표현임. 좀 더 실감나게 의역을 하면 "** (** = 6 X 3)! 너 누구야?"라는 뉘앙스에 가깝습니다. 영화나 미드에서 워낙 많이 나오는 표현이라서 한 번 소개해 보았습니다. 건강하게 오래 사시기를 바란다면 실제 대화에서는 "Who are you?"를 사용하시길..)

03 부사 역할 ① 목적

My father works hard to support his family. I study hard to pass the math test. My mother prepares the meal to make us happy.

Yesterday I went to the library to return a book. My mom went to the supermarket to buy some fruits. My dad went to the office to earn money.

I saw her two months ago. I fell in love with her at first sight. I came here to see her. She came here to see me, too. I was going to say something to her. But she didn't wait. She talked to me first.

03 부사 역할 ② 원인

What? You passed the math test? I am very happy to hear the good news.

What? You failed the math test? I am sorry to hear the bad news.

I thought I failed the test. So I was surprised to get an A on the test.

단어 및 숙어

buy [bai] 사다
earn [ərn] 일하여 벌다
fail [feil] 실패하다
fall [fɔ:l] / fell [fel] / fallen [fɔ:ln]
떨어지다
fruit [fru:t] 과일
library [ˈlaibrəri] 도서관, 도서실
math [mæθ] 수학
meal [mi:l] 식사, 한 끼
office [ˈɔ:fis] 사무실
pass [pæs] 통과하다, 지나가다
prepare [priˈpeər] 준비하다, 준비시키다
return [riˈtərn] 돌려주다, 돌아오다
see [si:] / saw [sɔ:] / seen [si:n] 보다

sight [sait] 광경, 경치
supermarket [ˈsu:pərmarkit] 슈퍼마켓
support [səˈpɔ:rt] 부양하다, 지지하다
wait [weit] 기다리다

at first sight 첫 눈에
be going to ~하려고 하다, ~할 예정이다
fail the math test
시험에 실패하다, 시험에 떨어지다
fall in love 사랑에 빠지다
get an A A학점을 받다
pass the math test
수학 시험에 합격하다, 수학 시험을 통과하다
pass the test 시험에 합격하다

해설

부사 역할
① **목적** : 본문의 밑줄은 모두 부정사의 부사적 용법으로 목적(~하기 위하여, ~하려고)의 의미이다.

My father works hard to support his family.
나의 아버지는 가족을 부양하기 위하여 열심히 일을 한다.

I went to the library to return a book.
책을 반납하기 위하여 도서관에 갔다.

I fell in love at first sight. I came here to see her
나는 첫눈에 사랑에 빠졌다. 나는 그녀를 보려고 여기에 왔다.

I was going to say something to her. But she didn't wait. She talked to me first.
나는 그녀에게 말을 하려고 했다. 그러나 그녀는 말할 틈을 주지 않았다.
(그녀는 기다리지 않았다.) 그녀가 나에게 먼저 말을 걸어왔다.

② **원인** : 본문의 밑줄은 모두 부정사의 부사적 용법으로 원인(~하다니, ~해서)의 의미이다.

I am very happy to hear the good news. 좋은 소식을 들어서 아주 기쁘다.
I was surprised to get an A on the test. 시험에서 A학점을 맞아서 놀랐다.

Nice to meet you! I am glad to meet you! Maybe you have not seen me before, but I know you. I have been always with you. You are so beautiful. You are so kind to everyone. You always made me happy. I was always happy to see you. I was always happy to see you in the street.

I saw you one day. You were crying in the street. You were crying like a baby. Your eyes were filled with tears. When I saw your eyes were filled with tears, my heart was broken. I was sad to see that sight. I could not sleep that night. But when I saw you the next day, you looked happy. I was so happy to see you smile again. Did I talk too much? I am sorry to make you feel uncomfortable. Who am I? I am your guardian angel*. Don't forget that I'm always with you.

* guardian angel [ˈgɑrdiən ˈeɪndʒəl] 수호천사

03 부사 역할 ③ 판단의 근거 (~하다니)

She told me that she did it and she was wrong. She must be honest to say so.

I think it's very difficult question. You must be a genius to solve the question easily.

단어 및 숙어

always [ˈɔːlweiz] 항상
broken [broukn] 깨진, 부서진
cry [krai] 울다
difficult [ˈdifikəlt] 어려운
easily [ˈiːzili] 쉽게
eye [ai] 눈
forget [fərˈget] 잊어버리다
genius [ˈdʒiːniəs] 천재
glad [glæd] 기쁜
guardian [ˈgardiən] 수호자, 후견인
heart [haːrt] 심장
honest [ˈanist] 정직한, 솔직한
kind [kaind] 친절한
maybe [ˈmeibi] 아마, 어쩌면
question [ˈkwestʃən] 문제, 질문
see [siː] / saw [sɔː] / seen [siːn]
sight [sait] 광경, 경치

solve [saːlv] 풀다, 해결하다
street [striːt] 거리
tear [tiər] 눈물
uncomfortable [ʌnˈkʌmpfərtəbl] 불편한
wrong [rɔːŋ] 틀린, 잘못된

glad to meet you 만나서 반갑습니다
guardian angel [ˈgardiən ˈeindʒəl] 수호천사
in the street 길거리에서
Nice to meet you 만나서 반갑습니다
must be ~임에 틀림없다
one day 어느 날
talk too much 말이 너무 많다
the next day 그 다음날

해설

② **원인** : 밑줄은 모두 부정사의 부사적 용법으로 원인(~하다니, ~해서)의 의미이다.

Nice to meet you! 당신을 만나서 좋다. → 만나서 반갑습니다.
I am glad to meet you! 당신을 만나서 기쁩니다. → 만나서 반갑습니다.
I have been always with you. 나는 항상 당신 곁에 있었습니다.
You are so kind to everyone. 당신은 모든 사람에게 정말 친절합니다.
I was always happy to see you. 당신을 보면 나는 항상 행복했습니다.
My heart was broken. 심장이 부서졌다. → 가슴이 찢어지는 것 같았다.
Did I talk too much? 말이 너무 많았나요?
Don't forget that I'm always with you. 내가 항상 곁에 있다는 것을 잊지 마세요.

③ **판단의 근거** (~하다니) : 본문의 밑줄은 모두 부정사의 부사적 용법으로 (~하다니)의 의미이다.

She must be honesty to say so. 그렇게 말하다니 그녀는 솔직한 사람이 틀림없다.
You must be a genius to solve the question easily. 그 문제를 쉽게 풀다니 너는 천재가 틀림없다.

What did he say to you? What? Did he say that to you? He cannot be rich to ask you for some money.

Tom made a mistake yesterday. And he made the same mistake today. Tom is stupid to make the same mistake again.

Tom is a liar. He is always telling lies. Mary is foolish to trust Tom.

03 부사 역할 ④ 조건 (만일 ~한다면)

What? Is it a lie? Don't tell a lie again. To tell a lie again, you will be punished.

What? Did you break the window? Don't do it again! To do it again, you will be punished.

Mary sings very well. To hear her sing, you would take her for a singer.

Tom speaks English very well. To hear him speak English, you would take him for an American.

단어 및 숙어

again [əˈgen] 다시, 또
always [ˈɔːlweiz] 항상
American [əˈmerikən] 미국인
ask [æsk] 부탁하다, 묻다
break [breik] 깨다, 부수다
foolish [ˈfuːliʃ] 어리석은
hear [hiər] 듣다 / heard [hərd] /
heard [hərd]
if [if] 만약 ~라면
liar [ˈlaiər] 거짓말쟁이
lie [lai] 거짓말하다
make [meik] 만들다 / made [meid] /
made [meid]
mistake [miˈsteik] 실수
money [ˈmʌni] 돈
punish [ˈpʌniʃ] 처벌하다

rich [ritʃ] 부유한
same [seim] 같은
sing [siŋ] 노래하다
singer [ˈsiŋər] 가수
speak [spiːk] 말하다
stupid [ˈstuːpid] 바보같은
trust [trʌst] 믿다
window [ˈwindou] 창문
would [wud] will(~할 것이다)의 과거

cannot be ~일리가 없다
break the window 창문을 깨다
make a mistake 실수를 하다
take A for B A를 B로 여기다
tell a lie(복수 tell lies)
거짓말하다(거짓말들을 하다)

해설

What did he say to you? 그가 당신에게 뭐라고 말했나요?
Did he say that to you? 당신에게 그렇게 말했나요?
He cannot be rich to ask you for some money. 당신에게 돈을 부탁하다니 그는 부자일 리가 없다.
Tom is stupid to make the same mistake again. 같은 실수를 또 하다니 톰은 바보다.
Mary is foolish to trust Tom. 톰을 믿다니 메리는 어리석다.

④ 조건 (만일 ~한다면)

To tell a lie again, you will be punished. 또 거짓말한다면 벌 받을 것이다.

To do it again, you will be punished. 또 한다면, 벌 받들 것이다.

To hear her sing, you would take her for a singer.
노래하는 것을 듣는다면 당신은 그녀를 가수라고 생각할 것이다.
(= If you heard her sing, you would take her for a singer.)

To hear him speak English, you would take him for an American.
영어로 말하는 것을 듣는다면 그를 미국 사람이라고 생각할 것이다.
(= If you heard him speak English, you would take him for an American.)

Oh Juliet! I would be happy to see you. I would be happy to meet you. I would be happy to take your hand. I would be happy to touch your cheek. I would be happy to kiss you. Oh Juliet! I would be happy to go with you. I would be happy to marry you. I would be happy even to die with you.

03 부사 역할 ⑤ 결과

She lived to be 36 years old. That means she died at the age of 36. And her mother lived to be 52 years old. She grew up to be a famous actress. She grew up to be the most popular actress in the world. One day, she woke up to find herself suddenly famous. She was the most popular actress in America. But there were no true friends around the actress.

One night, she woke up to find herself alone in the room. She opened the door only to find herself alone in the house. She was so lonely. Tears rolled down her cheeks. She took some medicine to sleep. But she took too much medicine. She slept and never to wake up again. She was 36 years old. Do you know who the actress is? Her name is Marilyn Monroe

* Marilyn Monroe ['mærəlin mən'rou] 마를린 먼로 1960년대 여배우

단어 및 숙어

actress [ˈæktris] 여배우
around [əˈraund] ~의 주변에
cheek [tʃiːk] 뺨
even [ˈiːvn] ~조차, 심지어
famous [ˈfeiməs] 유명한
grow [grou] / grew [gruː] / grown [groun]
Juliet [ˈdʒuːliet] 줄리엣, 여자 이름
lonely [ˈlounli] 외로운
marry [ˈmæri] 결혼하다
mean [miːn] 의미하다
medicine [ˈmedisin] 약
popular [ˈpaːpjulər] 인기 있는
sleep [sliːp] / slept [slept] / slept [slept]
suddenly [ˈsʌdnli] 갑자기
tear [tiər] 눈물
wake [weik] / woke [wouk] / woken [woukn] : 깨다, 일어나다
would [wud] will(~할 것이다)의 과거

at the age of ~의 나이에
die with ~와 함께 죽다
grow up 자라다
grow up to 자라서 ~이 되다
Marilyn Monroe 마를린 먼로(1960년대 금발의 미국 여자 배우)
only to 결과는 ~뿐인
roll down 굴러 내리다
take medicine 약을 먹다
take your hand 당신의 손을 잡다
true friend 진정한 친구
wake up (잠을)깨다, 정신을 차리다

해설

④ 조건 (만일 ~한다면)
본문의 밑줄은 전부 조건의 의미이다.

I would be happy to see you.
그대를 본다면 행복할 것입니다.

I would be happy to take your hand.
그대의 손을 잡는다면 행복할 것입니다.

I would be happy to go with you.
그대와 함께 간다면 행복할 것입니다.

I would be happy even to die with you.
설사 그대와 함께 죽어도 행복할 것입니다.

⑤ 결과
본문의 밑줄은 전부 결과의 의미이다.

She lived to be 36 years old.
그녀는 살았다.(She lived) 그 결과 36살이 되었다.(to be 36 years old.) →
그녀는 36살까지 살았다.

That means she died at the age of 36.
그것은 그녀가 36살에 죽었다는 것을 의미한다.

She grew up to be a famous actress.
그녀는 자랐다. (She grew up) 그 결과 유명한 여배우가 되었다.(to be a famous actress.) →
그녀는 자라서 유명한 여배우가 되었다.

One day she woke up to find herself suddenly famous.
어느 날 그녀는 깨어났다.(She woke up) 그 결과 그녀 자신이 갑자기 유명해진 것을 발견하였다. →
그녀는 어느 날 깨어보니 갑자기 유명해져 있었다.

She opened the door only to find herself alone in the house.
그녀는 문을 열었으나 집에 단지 자신 혼자만 있다는 것을 알았다.

Tears rolled down her cheeks.
눈물이 뺨에 흘러 내렸다.

She took some medicine to sleep.
그녀는 잠들기 위해서 약을 (수면제)를 먹었다.

She slept and never to wake up again.
잠들어서 다시는 깨어나지 못했다.

04 be + to 부정사 ① 명사 역할

To see is to believe. To see something <u>is to</u> believe something.
The teacher's job is to teach students. And the student's job <u>is to</u> learn.

04 be + to 부정사 ② 형용사 역할

(01) 예정
Mary <u>is to</u> arrive in this city at 7 p.m. Tom <u>is to</u> arrive at the station at 7:30 p.m. And we <u>are to</u> meet them at the station. So we <u>are to</u> leave house at 6 p.m. We <u>are to</u> meet them at 7:40 p.m.

(02) 의무
I know you are a good student. So you <u>are to</u> obey your mother. Your mother said, "Finish your homework by eight. And clean your room before you go to bed. And then, go to bed early." So you <u>are to</u> finish your homework by eight. And you <u>are to</u> clean your room before you go to bed. And then you <u>are to</u> go to bed early.

단어 및 숙어

arrive [əˈraiv] 도착하다
believe [biˈli:v] 믿다
city [ˈsiti] 도시
eight [eit] 여덟, 8
finish [ˈfiniʃ] 끝나다, 끝내다
leave [li:v] 떠나다

obey [ouˈbei] 복종하다, 따르다
station [ˈsteiʃən] 역

arrive at ~에 도착하다
by eight 여덟 시까지

해설

be + to 부정사

① 명사 역할

To see something is to believe something.
무언가를 보는 것은 무언가를 믿는 것이다. → 보면 믿는다.

② 형용사 역할

1) 예정 : ~할 예정이다.
본문의 밑줄은 전부 예정의 의미이다.

Mary is to arrive in this city at 7 p.m.
메리는 이 도시에 7시에 도착할 예정이다.

So we are to leave house at 6 p.m.
그래서 우리는 6시에 집을 떠날 예정이다.

2) 의무 : ~해야 한다.
본문의 밑줄은 전부 의무의 의미이다.

You are to obey your mother.
너는 너의 엄마의 말에 따라야 한다. (복종해야 한다.)

And you are to clean your room before you go to bed.
그리고 너는 잠자기 전에 너의 방을 치워야 한다.

(03) 의도

If you are to succeed, you must work hard. If you are to earn a lot of money, you must work hard. If you are to eat something, wash your hands first. If you are to make friends, be a good boy first.

(04) 운명

He left his home to earn money. When he said goodbye to his wife, he thought he would see her again. But he was never to see her again. He did not know it at that time. When he left his home, he thought he could return home. But he was never to return home. He did not know it at that time. When he left his country, he said to himself, "I will make a lot of money in America. And I will come back to my country." But he was never to come back to his country.

(05) 가능

There is no one in the street. I mean, no one was to be seen in the street.

It was midnight without the moon. And it rained a lot. So nothing was to be seen.

단어 및 숙어

country [ˈkʌntri] 나라, 시골
earn [ərn] 돈 등을 벌다.
himself [himˈself] 자신
leave [li;v] / left [left] / left [left]
midnight [ˈmidnait] 자정, 한밤중
moon [mu:n] 달
nothing [ˈnʌθiŋ] 아무것도
rain [rein] 비, 비가 오다
return [riˈtərn] 돌아오다, 돌아가다
succeed [səkˈsi:d] 성공하다
think [θiŋk] / thought [θɔ:t] / thought [θɔ:t]
without [wiˈðaut] ~없이

a lot 많은
a lot of 많은
at that time 그때에는
come back to ~로 돌아오다
make friends 친구를 사귀다
midnight without the moon
달도 없는 한밤중
say goodbye to ~에게 작별인사를 하다
say to oneself
속으로 말하다, 혼잣말하다

해설

3) 의도 : ~하려면
본문의 밑줄은 전부 의도의 의미이다.

If you are to succeed, you must work hard. 성공하려면 열심히 일해야 한다.

4) 운명 : ~할 운명이었다.
본문의 밑줄을 그은 것은 모두 운명의 의미이다.

He left his home to earn money. (목적) 돈을 벌기 위하여 집을 떠났다.
But he was never to see her again. 그는 그녀를 다시는 보지 못할 운명이었다.
But he was never to return home. 그는 다시는 집으로 돌아오지 못할 운명이었다.
I mean no one was to be seen in the street.
내 말은 거리에(in the street) 한 사람도(one) 보일 수(was to be seen)가 없다(no)는 말이다. →
내 말은 거리에 아무도 보이지 않는다는 말이다.

There was no one in the house. There was nothing in the house. So not a sound was to be heard in the house.

There is a building near the park. So the building is to be seen from the park. I mean, you can see the building from the park.

05 원형 부정사 (to가 없는 부정사) ①
지각동사(사역동사) + 목적어 + 원형 부정사

Let me tell you... Let me tell you what happened last night. I saw Tom and Dick come into my house. Tom made Dick shut the door. I heard a man scream after they came into my house. It was my dad's voice. They came into my room. I felt something touch my body. I felt something come inside my body. It was cold and sharp. It was a knife. I was covered in blood. Dick helped Tom kill me. Dick helped Tom kill my dad. I watched them leave my house. I heard them sing a song. Tom killed me and my dad. And Dick helped Tom kill us. Both of us were covered in blood. Both of us were dead. I... was killed last night. But now I am talking to you.

Do you know who I am? I am.. a ghost. Ha ha ha.. It was just a dream. But the dream was really horrible. I think I have to stop watching horror movies.

단어 및 숙어

blood [blʌd] 피
building [ˈbildiŋ] 건물
cover [ˈkʌvər] 덮다, 뚜껑
ghost [goust] 유령
happen [ˈhæpn] 일어나다
hear [hiər] / heard [hərd] / heard [hərd]
horrible [ˈhɔːribl] 끔찍한
horror [ˈhɔːrər] 공포
knife [naif] 칼
leave [liːv] 떠나다, 남기고 가다
let [let] 허락하다 / ～하게 하다, 시키다
nothing [ˈnʌθiŋ] 아무것도
park [paːrk] 공원
see [siː] / saw [sɔː] / seen [siːn]

scream [skriːm] 소리치다, 비명을 지르다
sharp [ʃaːrp] 날카로운, 뾰족한
shut [ʃʌt] (문 등을) 닫다
song [sɔːŋ] 노래
touch [tʌtʃ] 닿다, 만지다
voice [vɔis] 목소리
watch [waːtʃ] 보다

ha ha ha 하 하 하 (웃음소리)
have to ～ 해야 한다
horror movies [ˈhɔːrər ˈmuːviz] 공포 영화
sing a song 노래를 부르다
stop ~ing ～하는 것을 그만두다

해설

So not a sound was to be heard in the house. 그래서 그 집에서는 무슨 소리도 들리지 않는다.

원형 부정사
① 지각동사(사역동사) + 목적어 + 원형 부정사 (to가 없는 부정사 : 동사 원형)

지각동사(see, hear, watch, feel 등)와 사역동사(let, make, have, help 등) 뒤에 지각동사(사역동사) + 목적어 + 목적 보어 (원형 부정사)의 형태로 to가 없는 동사 원형이 쓰인다. 단, help는 원형 부정사나 to 부정사 모두 가능하다.

had better나 can not but 같은 관용적 표현 다음에는 원형 부정사를 쓴다.

Let me tell you. 내가 말을 하도록 허락하세요. 말씀드리겠습니다.
Let me tell you what happened last night. 어젯밤에 무슨 일이 있었는지 말하겠습니다.
I heard a man scream after they came into my house.
그들이 집으로 들어온 다음에 남자의 비명소리가 들렸다.
I was covered in blood. 나는 온통 피범벅이 되었다.
I think I have to stop watching horror movies.
나는 생각한다.(I think) 공포 영화 보는 것을(watching horror movies) 그만(stop)두어야만 한다.
(have to) → 공포영화를 그만 보아야할 것 같아.

05 원형 부정사 (to가 없는 부정사) ②
had better + 원형 부정사

You look tired. You had better go home early.
You look sick. You had better stay in bed.
It is raining. You'd better stay here.

It's sunny and warm. You'd better not stay home. Go outside to take a walk or something.
"Mom, I'm going to the movies." "You have a test tomorrow. You'd better not go to the movies."

05 원형 부정사 (to가 없는 부정사) ③
can not but + 원형 부정사

We were waiting for Billy. But he didn't appear. Tom said to me, "Billy told me that he would not come. He told me that he could not leave his family behind." I had never seen Tom tell a lie before. Tom always told the truth. I could not but believe him. But I couldn't make up my mind easily. Tom said to me, "John, there is no time to hesitate. We have no choice. We must leave right now." I could not but accept it. We had to leave Billy behind. I could not but believe Tom at that time. But Tom lied to me.

단어 및 숙어

accept [əkˈsept] 받아들이다, 인정하다
appear [əˈpiər] 나타나다, 보이다
behind [biˈhaind] 뒤에
choice [ˈtʃɔis] 선택
hesitate [ˈheziteit] 주저하다, 망설이다
lie [lai] 거짓말, 거짓말하다
/ lied [laid] / lied [laid]
look [luk] ~처럼 보이다, 보다
must [mʌst] (조동사) ~해야 하다
outside [autˈsaid] 밖으로
rain [rein] 비, 비가 오다
stay [stei] 머물다
sunny [ˈsʌni] 화창한
tired [taiərd] 피곤한
tell [tel] / told [tould] / told [tould]
truth [truːθ] 진리, 사실
warm [wɔːrm] 따뜻한

at that time 그때에, 그 당시에
can not but ~하지 않을 수 없다
go to the movies 영화 보러 가다
had better ~해야 한다, 하는 편이 낫다
had to : have to(~해야 한다)의 과거
leave 목적어 behind ~를 두고 가다, ~를 뒤에 남겨두고 떠나다
make up one's mind 결심하다
or something ~따위, ~등등
right now 지금 당장
stay in bed 침대 안에 있다
take a walk 산책하다
tell a lie 거짓말을 하다
tell the truth 사실대로 말하다, 진실을 말하다
wait for ~를 기다리다
You'd better = You had better

해설

② **had better + 원형 부정사** : ~해야 한다. ~하는 편이 낫다.

→ 부정문 : had better not **+ 원형 부정사**

Go outside to take a walk or something. 밖에 나가 산책 같은 것이라도 좀 해라.
You'd better not go to the movies. 영화 보러 가지 않는 편이 좋겠다. 영화 보러 가지 마라.

③ **can not but + 원형 부정사** : ~하지 않을 수 없다.
He told me that he could not leave his family behind.
그는 나에게 말했다. 그는 그의 가족을 뒤에 남겨두고 떠날(leave his family behind) 수가 없다고(he could not) → 가족을 남겨두고 떠날 수 없다고 내게 말했다.

there is no time to hesitate. 망설이고 있을 시간이 없다.
We have no choice. 다른 방법(선택)이 없다.
We had to leave Billy behind. 우리는 빌리를 남겨두고 떠나야만 했다.

06 부정사의 의미상 주어

This morning, my mother told me to wake up. She told me to get up. And she told me to have breakfast. I told her to wait a minute. After breakfast, my mother told me to go to school. And she told me that she was going to be late. She asked me to clean the kitchen and do the dishes before she arrives at house.

07 for 목적격 (of + 목적격) to 부정사

(01) I went to bed late last night. So it was impossible for me to get up early in the morning.

(02) The question was difficult. So it was impossible <u>for</u> me to answer the question.

(03) She studied hard. So it was natural <u>for</u> her to pass the exam.

(04) He didn't study hard. So it was natural <u>for</u> him to fail the exam.

(05) A: You are very <u>kind</u> to help him. I mean, it is very kind <u>of</u> you to help him. B: Thank you. It's very <u>nice of</u> you to say so.

단어 및 숙어

arrive [əˈraiv] 도착하다
difficult [ˈdifikəlt] 어려운, 곤란한
dish [diʃ] 접시
exam [igˈzæm] 시험
fail [feil] 실패하다
impossible [imˈpɑsəbl] 불가능한
late [leit] 늦은, 늦게
minute [ˈmiːnit] (시간의 단위) 분, 순간
natural [ˈnætʃərəl] 당연한, 자연의
pass [pæs] 통과하다, 지나가다
question [ˈkwestʃən] 질문
tell [tel] / told [tould] / told [tould]
wait [weit] 기다리다

wake [weik] 깨다, 일어나다
go [gou] / went [went] / gone [gɔːn]

arrives at ~에 도착하다
do the dishes 설거지하다
fail the exam 낙제하다
get up 일어나다
go to bed 잠자리에 들다
pass the exam 시험에 합격하다, 시험을 통과하다
wait a minute 잠깐만 기다려요
wake up 잠을 깨다, 정신을 차리다

해설

부정사의 의미상 주어 : 부정사의 동작이나 상태의 주체가 되는 것을 부정사의 의미상 주어라고 한다. 이 의미상 주어는 문장에 나타나지 않는 경우도 많으며 이러한 문법적인 지식은 이제는 시험에도 나오지 않으니 설명은 참고만 하고 영어 문장을 이해하기만 하면 된다.

She told me to get up. 그녀는 나를(me) 일어나라고(to get up) 했다.
→ 그녀는 나에게 일어나라고 했다. (여기서 me가 to get up의 의미상 주어이다.)
She asked me to clean the kitchen and wash the dishes.
그녀는 나에게 부엌을 치우고 접시를 닦으라고 부탁하였다.

for 목적격 (of + 목적격) to 부정사 : 부정사의 의미상의 주어를 밝힐 필요가 있는 경우 for + 목적격 또는 of + 목적격의 형태로 의미상의 주어를 나타낸다.

it was impossible for me to get up early in the morning.
내가(for me) 아침에 일찍 일어나는 것은(to get up early in the morning) 불가능했다(impossible).
You are very kind to help him. I mean, it is very kind of her to help him.
그를 돕다니 너는 정말 친절하다. 내 말은 그를 도우니 너는 정말 친절하다는 말이다.
It's very nice of you to say so. 그렇게 말해주다니 참 좋다. (←너 참 멋지다.)

시험 연구 : 목적격 앞에 of를 쓰는 경우를 묻는 문제가 자주 출제된다.
사람의 성격 등을 나타내어 사람을 칭찬하거나 비난하는 경우 of를 쓴다.
사람을 칭찬하는 형용사 : kind, nice, clever, generous, polite 등
사람을 비난하는 형용사 : wrong, foolish, stupid, silly, rude 등

08 too ~ to 부정사, enough to 부정사

Tom was in his room reading a comic book. Tom's mom was in the kitchen preparing dinner. And his dad was in the living room watching TV.

Mom said to dad, "Honey, please help me." Dad answered, "Honey, I'm too old to work. Please ask Tom to help you." "Tom, please help me." "Mom, I'm sorry. I can't. I'm too young to work. Please ask dad to help you." "Tom..., your dad told me that he was too old to work. Tom, you are grown up enough to help me."

"Mom, sorry. I can't." "Okay... I... see. Then you can not have dinner tonight. You are too young to eat chicken." "Mom, I can help you now." "No, you are too young to help me." "Mom, I have suddenly grown enough to help you." Tom helped his mom. "OK, you did a good job. But you can't eat chicken." "Why not? I helped you." "Yes, you helped me. And you have grown enough to help me. But you are still too young to eat chicken."

단어 및 숙어

chicken [ˈtʃikin] 닭
comic [ˈkɑːmik] 만화의
dinner [ˈdinər] 저녁 식사
enough [iˈnʌf] 충분한, 넉넉한
grow [grou] 자라다 / grew [gruː] / grown [groun]
honey [ˈhʌni] 여보, 자기야
job [dʒɑːb] 일, 직업
kitchen [ˈkitʃin] 부엌, 주방
still [stil] 아직도, 여전히
suddenly [ˈsʌdnli] 갑자기, 별안간
tell [tel] / told [tould] / told [tould] 말하다
watch [wɑːtʃ] 보다

comic book 만화책
enough to ~하기에 충분하다
grow up 자라다
have dinner 저녁 식사를 하다
OK you did a good job
좋아! 잘했다(관용적인 표현)
too ~ to - 너무 ~해서 -할 수 없다, -하기에는 너무 ~하다

해설

too ~ to - : '너무 ~해서 - 하지 못하다.' '-하기에는 너무 ~ 하다.'
enough to : ~할 정도로 충분한

Tom was in his room reading a comic book.
Tom은 자기 방에서 만화책을 보고 있다. (← 방에 있다. 만화책을 읽으며)

Tom's mom was in the kitchen preparing dinner.
Tom의 엄마는 식당에서 저녁을 준비하고 있다. (← 부엌에 있다. 저녁을 준비하면서)

Honey, I'm too old to work. Please ask Tom to help you.
여보! 나는 너무 나이가 많아서 일을 할 수가 없어요. Tom에게 도와달라고 하세요.

I'm too young to work. 나는 일하기에는 너무 어려요.
Tom you are grown up enough to help me. 토..옴.. 너는 나를 도울 만큼 충분히 컸단다.
"Mom, I have suddenly grown enough to help you." 엄마 갑자기 엄마를 도울 만큼 자랐어요.

종합 이해

To learn is fun. To learn a language is fun. To learn is to become a better person. To learn English is to get more information. Information is power. Information is the key to power. To get more information is to get more power. To learn English is to become a more able man. To learn English is to become a more important man. We live in a global world. To learn English is to get more power in this global world.

I learn. I learn a language. I learn a foreign language. I learn English. I learn English fast. I learn English very fast. I learn English easily. I learn English fast and easily. I think that English is easy. I think that English is easy to learn. I think that English is not difficult. I think that English is not difficult to learn.

I think that English is an easy language. I think that English is an easy language to learn. I think that English is quite an easy language to learn. I think that English is not a difficult language. I think that English is not a difficult foreign language to learn. I think that it is easy to learn English. I think that it is easy to master English.

단어 및 숙어

able [ˈeibl] ~할 수 있는, 유능한
believe [biˈliːv] 믿다
good [gud] < better [ˈbetər] <
best [best] 더 나은
difficult [ˈdifikəlt] 어려운, 곤란한
easily [ˈiːzili] 쉽게
easy [ˈiːzi] 쉬운
foreign [ˈfɔːrən] 외국의
fun [fʌn] 재미있는
global [ˈgloubəl] 세계적인
important [imˈpɔːrtənt] 중요한
information [infərˈmeiʃən] 정보
key [kiː] 핵심, 열쇠
language [ˈlæŋgwidʒ] 언어

master [ˈmæstər] 통달하다, 달인
person [ˈpəːrsn] 사람
power [pauər] 권력, 힘
quite [kwait] 꽤, 아주

foreign language 외국어
get more information
더 많은 정보를 얻다
global world 지구촌 세상
information is the key to power
정보는 힘을 얻는 비결이다(← 정보는 힘을 얻는 열쇠이다)
quite an easy language 꽤 쉬운 언어

해설

To learn a language is fun. 영어를 배우는 것은 재미있다.

To learn English is to get more information.
영어를 배운다는 것은 더 많은 정보를 얻는다는 것이다. (영어를 배우면 더 많은 정보를 얻을 수 있다.)

Information is the key to power. 정보는 힘으로 가는 열쇠이다. (정보는 힘의 비결이다.)

To learn English is to get more power in this global world.
영어를 배운다는 것은 이 지구촌 시대에 더 많은 힘을 갖는 것이다.

I think that English is easy to learn. 영어는 배우기에 쉽다고 생각한다.

I think that English is quite an easy language to learn.
나는 영어가 배우기에(to learn) 꽤 쉬운 언어(quite an easy language)라고 생각한다.

I think that it is easy to learn English. 나는 그것(it), 영어를 배우는 것(to learn English)은 쉽다고 생각한다. (나는 영어는 배우기가 쉽다고 생각한다.)

As a foreign language, English is not difficult. As a foreign language, English is not difficult to learn. As a foreign language, English is easy to master. As a foreign language, English is an easy language to master.

I know you are studying hard to master English. And I'm watching you study hard to master English. If you are to master English, you just need to study hard. It's not difficult for you to master English. To master English is not as difficult as you think. <u>All you need to do</u> is <u>to keep going</u>.

Come on! Keep going!
Keep going just a little bit longer! I believe you will finish this book very soon. I hope you will finish this book as soon as possible and go to the next step.

단어 및 숙어

bit [bit] 조금 약간
easy [ˈiːzi] 쉬운
foreign [ˈfɔːrən] 외국의
language [ˈlæŋgwidʒ] 언어
longer [ˈlɔːŋgər]
더 오래 long(긴, 오래)의 비교급
master [ˈmæstər] 통달하다 / 달인, 스승
step [step] 단계, 걸음

All you need to do is ~ 당신은 ~ 하기만 하면 된다, 당신이 할일은 ~뿐이다
As a foreign language 외국어로서
as soon as passible 가능한 빨리
just a little bit longer 조금만 더
just need to ~하기만 하면 된다
keep going 계속해 나가다, 계속해서 가다
keep ~ing 계속해서 ~하다
very soon 곧, 조속히

해설

As a foreign language, English is not difficult to learn.
외국어로서 영어는 배우기에 어렵지 않다.

I know you are studying hard to master English.
(to master : 마스터하기 위하여) 영어에 통달하려고 열심히 하는 것을 안다.

If you are to master English, you just need to study hard.
(are to master : 마스터하려면) 영어에 통달하려면 열심히 하기만 하면 된다.

To master English is not as difficult as you think.
(To master English : 영어에 통달하는 것) 영어에 통달하는 것은 당신이 생각하는 것만큼 어렵지 않다.

All you need to do is to keep going.
그대가 필요한 할 일은 계속 나가는 것이다.
→ 그대는 그저 계속 가기만 하면 된다. (to keep going : 계속 나가는 것)

Keep going just a little bit longer.
조금만 더 합시다.

I hope you will finish this book as soon as possible and go to the next step.
가능한 빨리 이 책을 마치고 다음 단계로 가기를 바란다.

PART 09.
분사

01 현재분사

"What are you doing?" "I'm reading a book."

I saw a girl playing the piano. And I saw a boy sitting behind the piano. "Who is the girl playing the piano?" "The girl playing the piano is my sister." "And who is the boy sitting behind the piano?" "The boy sitting behind the piano is her boyfriend."

02 과거분사

The window was broken by me.
I have lived in Seoul since last year.

One day I was picking up some leaves fallen from the trees. Then I heard my name called behind me. He was a postman. I received a letter written in English. It was a letter written by Tom.

There was a man named Dick. He was born in 1980. He was born in a cold country. And there was a beautiful woman named Jane. She was born in 1982. She was born in a warm country. Dick was a cold-hearted man. However Jane was a warm-hearted woman. They met in New York in 2019. Take a guess! What happened? Nothing has happened. They were not interested in each other at all.

단어 및 숙어

bear [beər] / bore [bɔːr] / born [bɔːrn] 아이를 낳다
behind [biˈhaind] 뒤의, 뒤에
break [breik] / broke [brouk] / broken [broukn] 깨다, 부수다
country [ˈkʌntri] 나라, 시골
handsome [ˈhænsəm] 잘생긴
happen [ˈhæpn] ~한 일이 일어나다
hear [hiər] / heard [hərd] / heard [hərd] 듣다
hearted [haːrtid] ~한 마음을 가진
fall [fɔːl] / fell [fel] / fallen [fɔːln] 떨어지다
interested [ˈintərestid] 관심있는
leaves [liːvz] 나뭇잎(leaf [liːf])의 복수
meet [miːt] / met [met] / met [met] 만나다
nothing [ˈnʌθiŋ] 없음, 아무것도
pick [pik] 집다, 꺾다

postman [ˈpoustmən] 우편 배달부
receive [riˈsiːv] 받다
since [sins] ~이후, ~이래로
warm [wɔːrm] 따뜻한
write [rait] / wrote [rout] / written [writn] 쓰다

be born 태어나다
be interested in ~에 관심이 있다
cold-hearted [kould ˈhaːrtid] 냉정한
Take a guess! 알아 맞추어봐
not ~at all 전혀 ~이 아니다
Nothing has happened 아무 일도 일어나지 않았다
pick up 줍다, 집다
play the piano 피아노를 치다
warm-hearted [wɔːrm ˈhaːrtid] 마음이 따뜻한
What happened? 무슨 일이 일어났을까

해설

분사는 형용사의 역할을 한다. 동사의 원형에 ~ing를 붙인 현재분사는 능동과 진행의 의미(~하고 있는)가 있으며 과거분사는 수동과 완료의 의미(~하여진)가 있다.

현재분사

I'm reading a book. 나는 책을 읽고 있다. (현재 진행형)
I saw a girl playing the piano. And I saw a boy sitting behind the piano.
나는 피아노를 치고 있는 소녀를 보았다. 그리고 그 피아노 뒤에 앉아 있는 소년을 보았다.
The girl playing the piano is my sister. 피아노를 치고 있는 저 소녀는 나의 여동생이다.

과거분사

The window was broken by me. 창문은 나에 의해서 깨졌다. (수동태)
I have lived in seoul since last year. 지난해 이후로 서울에서 살아왔다. (현재완료)
There was a handsome man named Dick.
딕이라는 이름을 가진(딕이라고 이름이 지어진 : named) 잘생긴 남자가 있었다.
I was picking up some leaves fallen from the trees. 나무에서 떨어진 잎들을 줍고 있었다.
I heard my name called behind me. 뒤에서 내 이름이 불려지는 것을 들었다.
I received a letter written in English. 영어로 쓰인 편지를 받았다.

03 감정을 나타내는 동사

Today is Sunday. I do not go to work today. I am interested in books. So I read a book in the morning. It was a very interesting book. I am also interested in movies. So I went to the movies in the afternoon. The movie was very exciting. I was really excited.

He gave us a long speech. It was a boring speech. I was bored. I was really bored to hear his boring speech. I looked at Mary. Mary was bored to hear his boring speech, too.

단어 및 숙어

bore [bɔːr] 지루하다
boring [ˈbɔːrɪŋ] 지루한
excite [ikˈsait] 흥분시키다
excited [ikˈsaitid] 신이 난, 흥분한
exciting [ikˈsaitɪŋ] 흥분되는, 흥미진진한
give [giv] / gave [geiv] / given [givn] 주다
interested [ˈintərestid] 관심있는
interesting [ˈintərestɪŋ] 흥미로운
speech [spiːtʃ] 연설

be bored 지루함을 느끼다
be interested in ~에 관심이 있다
give a speech 연설하다
go to the movies 영화 보러 가다
go to work 출근하다, 일하러 가다
look at 쳐다보다
run away 도망가다

해설

감정을 나타내는 동사

interest, excite, surprise, embarrass, amaze 등과 같이 사람의 감정을 나타내는 동사는 분사로 자주 쓰인다.

주어가 사람일 경우에는 그러한 것에서 " ~한 감정을 느끼게 되는" 수동의 의미로 과거분사가 쓰이고 주어가 사람이 아닌 경우 "그러한 감정을 불러일으키는" 능동의 의미로 현재분사가 쓰인다.

I do not go to work today. 오늘은 출근하지 않는다.
I am interested in books. 책에 관심이 있다. (독서를 좋아한다.)
The movie was very exciting.
영화가 나를 흥분시켰다. → 능동의 의미 → 현재분사 (영화는 흥미 진진 하였다.)
I was really excited.
나는 영화 때문에 흥분했다. → 수동의 의미 → 과거분사 (나는 정말 흥분했다.)
I was really bored to hear his boring speech.

04 분사구문 ① 시간

(01) 일반 문장

After I had finished my work, I left the building to go home. While I was walking along the street, I saw a boy. He looked very happy. When he saw me, he ran away. Who was he? Take a guess!

(02) 분사구문

Having finished my work, I left the building to go home. Walking along the street, I saw a boy. Seeing me, he ran away. He was my son. He left home without saying a word. I have never seen him after he left home. If he returns home, I will beat him up. Yes! I am a bad father! But do you know what happened?

단어 및 숙어

along [əˈlɔːŋ] ~을 따라서
beat [biːt] 때리다, 두드리다
building [ˈbɪldɪŋ] 건물, 건축
finish [ˈfɪnɪʃ] 끝내다
guess [ges] 추측하다, 짐작하다
return [rɪˈtɜrn] 돌아오다, 반납하다
without [wɪˈðaʊt] ~없이

beat up 두들겨 패다
take away 가지고 가다
Take a guess! 알아 맞춰봐!
walk along the street 길을 걷다
without saying a word 말없이

해설

분사구문
① 시간

분사구문이란 접속사 + 주어 + 동사 로 되어 있는 부사절을 분사를 이용하여 간결하게 나타내는 구문이다. 분사구문은 시간, 이유, 조건, 양보, 동시동작(부대상황) 등의 의미를 갖는다.

Having finished my work, I left the building to go home. (시간)
= After I had finished my work, I left the building to go home.
일을 끝마치고 나는 집으로 가기 위해서 그 빌딩을 떠났다. (to go : 부정사의 부사적 용법 (목적))

Walking along the street, I saw a boy. (시간)
= While I was walking along the street, I saw a boy.
길을 걷다가 한 소년을 보았다.

Seeing me, he ran away. (시간)
= When he saw me, he ran away.
그 소년은 나를 보자 도망쳤다.

04 분사구문 ② 원인 이유

(01) 일반 문장

I could not take a bus. That's because I had no money. I walked and walked to go home. Since I was tired, I could not walk any more. Since I was hungry, I could not walk any more. I could not eat anything all day long. That's because I had no money. Why did I have no money? Do you want to know more about it? Okay, I'll tell you about it.

(02) 분사구문

Having no money, I couldn't take a bus. I walked and walked to go home. Being tired, I couldn't walk any more. Being hungry, I couldn't walk any more. Having no money, I couldn't eat anything all day long. Leaving home, my son took away a lot of money! Leaving home, he took away all the money. He took away all the money that my family had!

Now do you understand why I was so angry? If he returns home, I will beat him up.

단어 및 숙어

as [æz] ~ 때문에 / ~로서
beat [bi:t] 때리다, 두드리다
couldn't ['kudnt] can not(~을 할 수 없다)의 과거인 could not의 줄인 말
hungry ['hʌŋgri] 배고픈
return [ri'tərn] 돌아오다 / 반납하다
Since [sins] ~이니까 / ~한 이래로
tired [taiərd] 피곤한
understand [ʌndər'stænd] 이해하다, 알다

all day long 하루 종일
any more 더 이상
beat up 구타하다, (흠씬) 두들겨 패다
take a bus 버스를 타다
take away 가지고 가다
That's because 그것은 ~ 때문이다

해설

② 원인 이유

본문에 밑줄을 그은 것은 전부 원인(~ 때문에)의 의미이다.

Having no money, I couldn't take a bus. = Because I had no money, I couldn't take a bus.
돈이 없어서 버스를 탈 수 없었다.

Being tired, I couldn't walk any more. = Since I was tired, I could not walk any more.
피곤해서(Since I was tired = As I was tired : 현대 영어 구어체에서는 As보다 Since를 더 많이 쓰므로 본문에서도 Since를 사용했음) 더 걸을 수 없었다.

* As는 다양한 기능과 뜻이 있는데 접속사 편에서 자세히 다룬다.

Being hungry, I couldn't walk any more. = Since I was hungry, I could not walk any more.
배가 고파서(Since I was hungry) 더 걸을 수 없었다.

Leaving home, my son took away a lot of money! Leaving home, he took away all the money. He took away all the money that my family had!
(여기서 Leaving home은 둘 다 모두 시간의 의미이다.)
집을 떠날 때 나의 아들은 많은 돈을 가지고 갔다. 집을 떠날 때 그는 모든 돈을 가지고 갔다. 그는 내 가족이 가진(what my family got) 모든 돈을 가지고 갔다.

04 분사구문 ③ 조건

(01) 일반 문장

But we need money. If he returns home early, he will not be beaten. If he returns home with the money, he will not be beaten. If he returns home without the money, he will be beaten to death. Ah, if I take a few step forward, I can see my house. Ah.. if I take one more step, I can see my house. Ah.... I'm... starving. I could eat a horse. I can't walk any more.

(02) 분사구문

Returning home early, he will not be beaten. Returning home with the money, he will not be beaten. Returning home without the money, he will be beaten to death. Taking a few step forward, I can see my house. Taking one more step forward, I can see my family. Ah... I'm starving. I could eat a horse.

04 분사구문 ④ 양보

(01) 일반 문장

Although I have a family, I can't meet my son. Although I live with my family, I can't see my son. Although I accept what my son did, I will not forgive him.

단어 및 숙어

accept [əkˈsept] 인정하다, 받아들이다
Although [ɔːlˈðou]
비록 ~라 할지라도, 비록 ~이긴 하지만
beat [biːt] / beat [biːt] /
beaten [biːtn] 때리다
corner [ˈkɔːrnər] 모퉁이, 구석
death [deθ] 죽음
forgive [fərˈgiv] 용서하다
forward [ˈfɔːrwərd] 앞으로
horse [hɔːrs] 말
need [niːd] 필요로 하다
return [riˈtəːrn] 돌아오다 / 반납하다
starve [staːrv] 굶주리다, 굶어죽다
step [step] 발걸음
turn [təːrn] 돌다, 돌리다
without [wiˈðaut] ~없이

a few 조금
any more 더 이상
be beaten to death 맞아죽다
(← 죽을 때까지 맞다 ←죽음까지 매를 맞다)
be beaten 매를 맞다
could eat a horse 배가 엄청 고프다
(너무 배고파서 말 한 마리를 다 먹을 수 있다)
I'm starving 배고파 죽겠다
live with ~와 함께 살다
not any more 더 이상 ~하지 않다
one more step 한 걸음 더
take a step forward
한 걸음 앞으로 더 나가다
take one more step forward
한 걸음 더 앞으로 나가다

해설

③ 조건

If I take a few step forward, 몇 발짝만 앞으로 더 나가면,

본문의 밑줄은 전부 조건(~하면 ~이라면)의 의미이다.

Returning home early, he will not be beaten.
= If he returns home early, he will not be beaten.
집에 일찍 돌아온다면 맞지 않을 것이다.

Returning home with the money, he will not be beaten.
= If he returns home with the money, he will not be beaten.

Taking a few step forward 몇 걸음만 앞으로 나아가면
Taking one more step 한 걸음만 더 나가면
Ah... I'm starving. I could eat a horse. 아 배고파 죽겠다. (너무 배고파서) 말 한 마리도 먹을 수 있겠다.

(02) 분사구문

<u>Having</u> a family, I can't meet my son. <u>Living</u> with my family, I can't see my son. I live without my son who stole my money. Although <u>accepting</u> what my son did, I will not forgive him.

05 분사구문 ⑤ 부대상황 (동시동작)

(01) 일반 문장

Finally, my son returned home. "Mom I'm home," he said while he was coming into the house. He smiled brightly, as he held out his arms to me. He left home a month ago and he returned home last night. He looked tired. He looked hungry. He had been at a homeless shelter for a month. He asked me, "Dad! Are you ok?"

(02) 분사구문

At last my son returned home last night. He came in the house <u>saying</u>, "Mom, I'm home." He held out his arms to me <u>smiling</u> brightly. He left home a month ago and he returned home last night. He asked, "Dad! Are you ok?" I answered <u>hugging</u> my son. "Yes, I'm ok. I have done it. But I could not have done it without your help. Thank you my son. Where have you been?" He answered, "I have been at a homeless shelter."

단어 및 숙어

accept [əkˈsept] 인정하다, 받아들이다
Although [ɔːlˈðou] 비록 ~라 할지라도, 비록 ~이긴 하지만
arm [aːrm] 팔
as [æz] ~하면서 / ~로서
brightly [ˈbraitli] 밝게, 환하게
finally [ˈfainəli] 마침내
forgive [fərˈgiv] 용서하다
hold [hould] / held [held] / held [held]
homeless [ˈhoumlis] 집이 없는
shelter [ˈʃeltər] 보호소, 피난처
hug [hʌg] 껴안다
hungry [ˈhʌŋgri] 배고픈
leave [liːv] / left [left] / left [left]
look [luk] ~처럼 보이다, 보다
month [mʌnθ] 달, 월

steal [stiːl] / stole [stoul] / stolen [stouln] 훔치다
tired [taiərd] 피곤한
without [wiˈðaut] ~없이

a month ago 한 달 전
at last 마침내
come in 들어오다
hard job 어려운 일
homeless shelter 노숙자 보호소
hold out (손 팔 등을) 내밀다
I'm home. 다녀왔습니다, 저 왔어요 (집에 올 때 하는 인사말)
last night 어젯밤
live with ~와 함께 살다
live without ~ 없이 살다

해설

④ **양보** : 비록 ~라 할지라도, 비록 ~이긴 하지만
본문의 밑줄은 전부 양보의 의미이다.
Having a family, I can't meet my son. = Although I have a family, I can't meet my son.
나는 가족이 있지만 아들을 만날 수는 없다.

Although accepting what my son did, I will not forgive him.
= Although I accept what my son did, I will not forgive him.
설사 내 아들이 한 일(what my son did)을 인정하더라도 용서하지는 않을 것이다.

⑤ **부대상황(동시동작)** : ~하면서
He came in the house saying, Mom I'm home.
= As he said, "Mom I'm home." he came in the house.
"엄마 저 왔어요."라고 말하면서 그는 집으로 들어왔다.

He held out his arms to me smiling brightly.
= As he smiled brightly, he held out his arms to me.
밝게 웃으면서 그는 나에게 그의 두 팔을 뻗었다. (두 팔을 벌렸다.)

But I could not have done it without your help.
그러나 너의 도움이 없었다면 나는 해내지 못했을 것이다.

05 분사구문 ⑤ 부대상황 (동시동작)

(03) 독해 연습

I have tried to stop drinking. But I failed many times. So my wife told my son. My wife told my son to take all the money and go out. She said to him, "If there is no money, your dad will not be able to buy alcohol." I heard that story before my son returned. Since I didn't drink for a month, she called him to return home. He has been at a homeless shelter.

단어 및 숙어

alcohol [ˈælkəhɔːl] 술, 알콜
buy [bai] 사다, 구입하다
call [kɔːl] 전화하다, 부르다
fail [feil] 실패하다
hear [hiər] / heard [hərd] / heard [hərd]
homeless [ˈhoumlis] 집이 없는
shelter [ˈʃeltər] 보호소, 피난처
since [sins] ~이므로, ~이니까 / ~이후로

be able to = can ~을 할 수 있다
for a month 한 달 동안
homeless shelter 노숙자 보호소
many times 여러 번
stop drinking 술을 끊다

해설

I have tried to stop drinking.
술을 끊으려고 노력해왔다.

My wife told my son to take all the money and go out.
나의 아내는 모든 돈을 가지고 (집을) 나가라고 내 아들에게 말했다.

If there is no money, your dad will not be able to buy alcohol.
만약 돈이 없으면 너의 아빠는 술을 살 수 없을 것이다.

Since I didn't drink for a month, she called him to return home.
내가 한 달 동안 술을 마시지 않자(않았기 때문에) 그녀는 그에게 집으로 돌아오라고 전화했다.

PART 10.
강조

01 Do를 사용한 강조

(01) 일반 문장

Come in and sit down. You know who broke the window. Tell me who broke the window.

(02) 강조 문장

I said, "Come in and sit down." He came in but he didn't sit down. I said again, "<u>Do</u> sit down!" He sat down. I said, "You <u>do</u> know who broke the window. <u>Do</u> tell me who broke the window."

02 It is ~ that 강조 구문

Jane was killed last night. I was in the park at that time. Her house is far from the park. I was taking a walk in the park. I met Mike then and there. He loved Jane so much. The police arrested Mike this morning. The police suspected that he killed her. I didn't understand why the police arrested him. I didn't understand why the police suspected him. So I went to the police station.

단어 및 숙어

arrest [əˈrest] 체포하다
break [breik] / broke [brouk] / broken [broukn]
far [fa:r] 멀리
meet [mi:t] / met [met] / met [met]
park [pa:rk] 공원
police [pəˈli:s] 경찰
sit [sit] / sat [sæt] / sat [sæt]
station [ˈsteiʃən] 역, 정거장
suspect [səˈspekt] 의심하다
understand [ʌndərˈstænd] 이해하다

at that time 그때, 그 당시에
far from ~에서 먼
in the park 공원에서
police station 경찰서
sit down 앉다
take a walk 산책하다
then and there 그때 그곳에서
this morning 오늘 아침
was killed 살해되었다(수동태 과거)

해설

Do를 사용한 강조

do 동사를 일반 동사 앞에 놓아 문장 내용을 강조하거나 명령의 뜻을 강조한다.
"분명히, 확실히, 제발, 바로" 등의 의미로 해석할 수 있다.

You know who broke the window. 너는 누가 창문을 깨뜨렸는지를 안다.
You do know who broke the window. 너는 누가 창문을 깨뜨렸는지를 분명히 안다.
Tell me who broke the window. 누가 창문을 깨뜨렸는지를 나에게 말해라.
Do tell me who broke the window. 누가 창문을 깨뜨렸는지를 말하란 말이야.

It is ~ that 강조 구문

강조하는 내용을 It is ~ that 사이에 두어 강조의 의미를 나타낸다.
that 대신에 다른 관계대명사를 쓰기도 한다.

Jane was killed last night. (수동태 과거) 제인은 어젯밤에 살해되었다.
I didn't understand why the police arrested him.
나는 왜 경찰이 그를 체포했는지 이해할 수가 없었다.

A cop asked me some questions in the police station.

"Did you say that Mike didn't kill Jane?"

"Yes, I did."

"Why do you think so?"

"It was I that(who) met him in the other place. So he has an alibi"

"Who did you meet yesterday?"

"It was Mike that (who) I met yesterday."

"Where did you meet him?"

"It was in the park that I met him yesterday. It's far from the house."

"When did you meet him"

"It was last night that I met him."

The cop asked me the last question.

"Are you sure?'

"Yes, I am. I'm sure."

The cop didn't ask me any more questions. I came back home from the police station. Mike got out of the police station the next day. But Mike didn't look happy. He said, "When Jane was dead, I was dead too."

단어 및 숙어

alibi [ˈælibai] 알리바이, 현장 부재 증명
(범죄가 일어난 곳에 있지 않았다는 증거)
cop [ka:p] 경찰
dead [ded] 죽은
far [fa:r] 멀리
get [get] / got [gat] / got [gat]
look [luk] ~처럼 보이다, 보다
meet [mi:t] / met [met] / met [met]
park [pa:rk] 공원
police [pəˈli:s] 경찰
question [ˈkwestʃən] 질문
station [ˈsteiʃən] 역, 정거장
sure [ʃuər] 확실한, 확신하는

far from ~에서 먼
get out of ~을 나오다, ~을 떠나다
I'm sure 확신하다, 틀림없다
in the other place 다른 장소에서
in the park 공원에서
last question 마지막 질문
police station 경찰서

해설

It was I that met him in the other place.
= It was I who met him in the other place.
그를 다른 장소에서 만난 사람이 바로 나다.

It was Mike that I met yesterday.
= It was Mike who I met yesterday.
내가 어제 만난 사람은 마이크이다.

Are you sure?
확실합니까? 정말입니까?

Mike got out of the police station.
마이크는 경찰서에서 나왔다.

When Jane was dead, I was dead too.
제인이 죽었을 때 나도 역시 죽었다.

독해 연습

I stood by the window. There was a chair near the window. I sat down on the chair. Sitting on the chair, I looked down the street. I looked down the street for a long time. I looked down the street for a long time without saying a word. I looked down the street through the window. There were a lot of couples. There were a lot of couples in the street. They love each other. And they will miss each other when they are far apart.

But they will hate each other. They will hate each other someday soon. Life is short and love is short, too. Life is too short to love enough. Just to be with a lover is enough. That was all that we wanted. That was all that we wanted from our lovers at first. But we want too many things from our lovers. That is not love. Love is not that kind of thing. That is just greed*. We meet because of love. And we part because of greed. * greed [griːd] 탐욕

I stood up. And I started to write a letter. I started to write a letter to my wife. 'I am sorry. It was my fault. It was a big mistake. I made a big mistake. Please forgive me. I will return to you. I will return to you right now. I will return to you right here right now. I will return to you before you receive this letter. I love you. I do love you. I will love you for the rest of my life....'

단어 및 숙어

apart [əˈpaːrt] 따로, 떨어져
chair [tʃeər] 의자
enough [iˈnʌf] 충분히, 충분한
far [faːr] 멀리
fault [fɔːlt] 잘못
forgive [fərˈgiv] 용서하다
greed [griːd] 탐욕
hate [heit] 미워하다
just [dʒʌst] 단지, 방금
kind [kaind] 종류 / 친절한
look [luk] ~처럼 보이다, 보다
miss [mis] 그리워 하다 / 놓치다
mistake [miˈsteik] 실수
part [paːrt] 헤어지다 / 부분
receive [rɪˈsiːv] 받다
rest [rest] 나머지
sit [sit] / sat [sæt] / sat [sæt]
soon [suːn] 곧
stand [stænd] / stood [stud] / stood [stud]
through [θruː] ~을 통하여
word [wəːrd] 말, 단어

at first 처음에
because of ~ 때문에
by the window 창가에
far apart 멀리 떨어져
for a long time 오랫동안
for the rest of my life 평생동안
make a big istake 큰 실수를 하다
make a mistake 실수를 하다
on the chair 의자 위에
right here 지금 여기서
right now 지금 당장
sit down 앉다
someday soon 가까운 날에, 언젠가 곧
stand up 일어서다
start to ~하기 시작하다
that kind of thing 그런 것
that kind of 그런, 그런 종류의
through the window 창문을 통하여
too ~ to 너무 ~해서 ~하지 못하다
without saying a word 한마디 말도 없이

해설

Sitting on the chair, I looked down the street.
의자에 앉아서 거리를 내려다보았다. (분사구문 동시동작)

I looked down the street for a long time without a word.
나는 말없이 오랫동안 거리를 내려다보았다.

And they will miss each other when they are far apart.
떨어져 있으면 서로를 그리워할 것이다.

Life is too short to love enough.
충분히 사랑하기에는 인생은 너무 짧다.

Just to be with a lover is enough.
단지 연인과 함께 있는 것(to be with a lover)만으로 충분하다.

That was all what we wanted from our lovers at first.
그것이 처음에 우리의 연인들에게(from our lovers) 우리가 원했던(what we wanted) 전부였다.

Love is not that kind of thing. That is just greed. We meet because of love. And we part because of greed.
사랑은 그런 것이 아니다. 그것은 단지 탐욕일 뿐이다.
우리는 사랑 때문에 만나서 탐욕 때문에 헤어진다.

I started to write a letter to my wife.
나는 아내에게 편지를 쓰기 시작했다.

I made a big mistake.
큰 실수를 했다.

I will return to you right now right here.
지금 당장 여기서 당신에게 돌아가겠어요.

I love you. I do love you.
사랑합니다. 정말 사랑합니다.

I will love you for the rest of my life.
평생 동안 당신을 사랑하겠습니다.

But... I could not write any more. I could not return to her. It was just my will*. *will [wil] 유언장

I cried. My eyes were filled with tears. Tears came out. Tears were rolling down my cheeks. My heart was broken. I killed my wife. I thought it was my anger that made me kill her. But it was my greed that made me kill her. When my wife was dead I was dead, too. I didn't kill my wife. I did kill myself. I opened the window. I took off my shoes. I stood on the chair. I looked down the street. It was the last minute in my life. Then, the phone was ringing.

I hesitated to answer the phone. It was the last phone call in my life. I hesitated for a while. But I decided to answer the phone. It was Mike. He said, "Your wife wasn't dead. She is alive. And she knew that you struck her just one time. She knew that you didn't mean to kill her. She told me that she would forgive you. And she said that you should come back home as soon as possible. Return to your home right now!"

단어 및 숙어

alive [əˈlaiv] 살아있는
break [breik] / broke [brouk] / broken [broukn]
chair [tʃeər] 의자
cheek [tʃi:k] 뺨
dead [ded] 죽은
forgive [fərˈgiv] 용서하다
greed [gri:d] 탐욕
heart [ha:rt] 심장, 가슴
hen [ðen] 그때, 그 다음에
hesitate [ˈheziteit] 망설이다, 주저하다
just [dʒʌst] 단지, 막
kind [kaind] 종류/ 친절한
know [nou] / knew [nju:] / known [noun]
mean [mi:n] 의미하다, 의도하다
phone [foun] 전화, 전화기
possible [ˈpa:səbl] 가능한
ring [riŋ] 울리다. / 반지
shoes [ʃu:z] 신발
should [ʃud] ~해야 한다
soon [su:n] 곧
stand [stænd] / stood [stud] / stood [stud]
strike [straik] / struck [strʌk] / struck [strʌk]
tear [tiər] 눈물
will [wil] 유언장 / ~을 할 것이다

answer the phon 전화를 받다
as soon as possible 가능한 빨리
be filled with ~로 가득하다
come out 나오다
decide to ~하기로 결정하다
didn't mean to 고의로 ~한 것이 아니다, ~할 의도가 아니었다
for a while 잠시동안
hesitate to ~하기를 망설이다
mean to ~할 작정이다, 의도적으로 ~하다
one time 한 번
phone call 통화, 전화통화
roll down my cheeks 뺨위로 흘러내리다
roll down 굴러 내리다
stand on ~위에 서다
take off (옷 등을) 벗다
the last minute 마지막 순간

해설

It was just my will.
그것은 단지 나의 유서일 뿐이다.

Tears were rolling down my cheeks. My heart was broken.
눈물이 뺨에 흘러내렸다. 가슴이 찢어지는 것 같았다.

I thought that it was my anger that made me kill her.
(It is ~ that 강조 구문) 그녀를 죽이도록 만든 것은 바로 나의 분노였다고 생각했다.

I didn't kill my wife. I did kill myself.
(do를 사용한 강조 구문) 나는 내 아내를 죽인 것이 아니다. 나는 바로 내 자신을 죽인 것이다.

It was the last minute in my life.
내 생애 마지막 순간이었다.

Then, the phone was ringing.
그때 전화벨이 울렸다.

I hesitated to answer the phone.
나는 전화 받기를 주저하였다.

It was the last phone call in my life.
그것은 내 생애 마지막 전화 통화였다.

She knew that you didn't mean to kill her.
그녀는 네가 그녀를 죽이려고 한 것은 아니었다는 것을 안다.

And she said you should come back home as soon as possible.
그리고 그녀는 네가 가능한 빨리 집으로 돌아와야 한다고 말했다.

Return to your home right now!
당장 집으로 돌아가라!

PART 11.
가정법

01 가정법 현재

If he is asleep, I will be awake. If he is awake, I will crawl. If he crawls, I will walk. If he walks, I will run. If he runs, I will fly.

02 가정법 과거

A student said, "Since I am not rich, I can not go to university. If I were rich, I could go to university." Is that true?

Do you think that only the rich can go to university? No, even though you are poor, you can go to university. If you studied hard, you could get a good grade. If you got a good grade, you could get a scholarship.

And if you were diligent, you could work part time. Of course, studying hard and working hard at the same time is not easy. But life is not an easy game. If you accepted the poor, you could learn lots of things from the poor. And the poor will make you a better person. No pain, no gain.

단어 및 숙어

accept [əkˈsept] 받아들이다, 인정하다
as [æz] ~때문에, ~이니까
asleep [əˈsliːp] 잠들어, 잠들은
awake [əˈweik] 깨어있는, 잠들지 않은
crawl [krɔːl] 기다, 포복하다
diligent [ˈdilidʒənt] 부지런한
easy [ˈiːzi] 쉬운
either [iːðər] 또한
fly [flai] 날다
gain [gein] 얻다
good [gud] < better [ˈbetər] < best [best]
grade [greid] 성적, 등급
pain [pein] 고통
person [ˈpəːrsn] 사람
scholarship [ˈskalərʃip] 장학금
since [sins] ~이므로, ~이니까 / ~이후로
though [ðou] ~일지라도, ~이긴 하지만
university [juːnɪˈvəːrsəti] 대학교

at the same time 함께, 동시에
even though 비록 ~일지라도
get a good grade 좋은 성적을 받다
go to university 대학에 다니다
lots of 많은
not ~ either ~또한 ~이 아니다
of course 물론
(the 형용사는 ①~한 사람들 ②추상명사의 뜻)
the poor 가난한 사람들 / 가난함
the rich 부자들 / 부유함
work part time 아르바이트를 하다, 시간제 근무를 하다

해설

가정법 현재
현재나 미래에 대한 가정을 하거나 상상을 나타낸다.

If + 주어 + 동사의 현재형, 주어 + will(can) + 동사원형 : 만일 ~ 한다면, ~ 할 것이다.

If he is asleep, I will be awake.
그가 잠들어 있으면 나는 깨어 있을 것이다.

If he crawls, I will walk.
그가 기어 다닌다면 나는 걸어 다닐 것이다.

가정법 과거
현재 사실에 반대되는 가정을 나타낸다.

If + 주어 + 동사의 과거형(be 동사의 경우 were), would(could should might) + 동사원형 :
만일 ~ 라면, ~ 할 것이다.

If I were rich, I could go to university.
= As I am not rich, I can not go to university.
만약 내가 부자라면 대학에 다닐 수 있을 것이다.

Do you think that only the rich can go to university?
단지 부자들만이(only the rich) 대학에 다닐 수 있다고 생각하세요?

If you studied hard, you could get a good grade.
만약 공부를 열심히 한다면, 좋은 성적을 받을 것이다.

studying hard and working hard at the same time is not easy.
      주어   동사 보어

공부를 열심히 하고 일을 열심히(studying hard and working hard) 동시에 (at the same time) 하는 것은 쉬운 일은 아니다.
→ 공부와 일을 동시에 다 열심히 하는 것은 쉬운 일은 아니다.

And the poor will make you better person.
그리고 가난(the poor)은 너를 더 나은 사람으로 만들어 줄 것이다.

No pain, no gain.
(속담) 고통 없이는 얻는 것도 없다. 노력 없이 얻는 것은 없다.

03 가정법 과거완료

I was born poor. But I'm rich and happy now. And I was happy even when I was poor. That's because I live in the present and watch the future. They say, "Poverty is the mother of crime." Yes, it is true. But that is not all.

Poverty is not always bad. <u>If</u> I <u>had not been</u> poor, I <u>could not have learned</u> lots of things. <u>If</u> I <u>had not learned</u> a lot of things in life, I <u>could not have succeeded</u>. <u>If</u> I <u>had not been</u> poor, I <u>would not have worked</u> hard. <u>If</u> I <u>had</u> not worked hard, I could not have succeeded. Above all, <u>if</u> I <u>had</u> not learned something in life, I would never have been happy.

I was born poor. My son was born rich. But my son doesn't look happy. I think it doesn't matter very much. I think it doesn't matter so much whether you are rich or not.

If you have something, you can enjoy it. If you don't have something, you can enjoy the process of getting it. I think life is a type of game. Of course, it is not an easy game. But what kind of game do you like? Too easy game or Not easy game? Keep this your mind! No pain, no gain. No pain, No pleasure.

단어 및 숙어

above [əˈbʌv] 위에
bear [beər] / bore [bɔ:r] / born [bɔ:rn]
crime [kraim] 범죄
future [ˈfju:tʃər] 미래
gain [gein] 획득, 얻다
kind [kaind] 종류, 친절한
learn [lə:rn] 배우다
look [luk] ~처럼 보이다, 보다
matter [ˈmætər] 중요하다, 문제
mind [maind] 마음, 정신
pain [pein] 고통
pleasure [ˈpleʒər] 기쁨, 즐거움
poverty [ˈpa:vərti] 가난, 빈곤
present [ˈpreznt] (형용사) 현재의 / 출석한 / 선물 / 주다, 선사하다
process [ˈprases] 과정, 절차
sort [sɔ:rt] 종류
succeed [səkˈsi:d] 성공하다
true [tru:] 사실인, 진실한
watch [wa:tʃ] 보다
whether [ˈweðər] ~인지 아닌지

a lot of 많은
a type of 일종의, ~같은 것
above all 무엇보다도, 특히
be born 태어나다(수동태)
it doesn't matter 그것은 중요하지 않다
Keep in your mind 명심해라, 기억해라
live in the present 현재에 살다
lots of 많은
of course 물론
Poverty is the mother of crime 가난은 범죄의 어머니, 가난이 죄다
so much 그렇게, 정말로
something like ~와 비슷한, ~같은 것
That's because 그것은 ~때문이다
the mother of crime 범죄의 어머니, 범죄의 근원
the present 현재
(the + 형용사는 ① ~한 사람들 ② 추상명사의 뜻)
try to ~하려고 노력하다
was born 태어났다 be born(태어나다)의 과거형

해설

가정법 과거완료 : 과거 사실에 반대되는 가정을 나타낸다.

If + had+과거분사 , would (could should might) + have+과거분사
만약 ~하였다면, ~했을 것이다.

I was born poor.
나는 가난하게 태어났다.

I was happy even when I was poor.
나는 가난할 때에도 행복했다.

No pain, no gain.
고통 없이는 얻는 것도 없다. 수고 없이 소득 없다.

No pain, No pleasure.
고통이 없으면 즐거움도 없다.

I live in the present and watch the future.
나는 현재에 살고 (live in the present) 미래를 본다.(watch the future) → 나는 항상 현실 속에서 현재에 충실히 살면서 미래를 바라보며 산다.

They say, "Poverty is the mother of crime." Yes, it is true. But that is not all.
사람들은 말한다. 가난이 범죄의 어머니라고. 물론 사실이다. 그러나 그것이 전부는 아니다. → 사람들은 말하기를 가난이 죄라고 한다. 물론 맞는 말이지만 항상 그런 것은 아니다.

Poverty is the mother of crime
(속담) 가난은 죄의 어머니이다. → 가난이 죄다. 빈곤이 범죄의 근원이다.

Poverty is not always bad. If I had not been poor, I could not have learned lots of things.
가난이 항상 나쁜 것만은 아니다. 만약 내가 가난하지 않았다면, 나는 많은 것들을 배우지 못했을 것이다.

I was born poor. My son was born rich. But my son doesn't look happy.
나는 가난하게 태어났고 내 아들은 부자로 태어났다. 그런데 내 아들이 행복해(happy.) 보이지 않는다.(doesn't look)

I think it doesn't matter very much whether you are rich or not.
나는 생각한다(I think) 당신이 부자인지 아닌지(whether you are rich or not.)는 대단히(very much) 중요 하지 않다(it doesn't matter)고
→ 나는 부자인지 아닌지는 그렇게 중요하지 않다고 생각한다.

If you have something, you can enjoy it. If you don't have something, you can enjoy the process of getting it.
(여기 if 절은 가정법이 아니라 단순히 조건문임)
만약 무엇을 가지고 있으면 그 가진 것을 즐길 수 있다. 만약 무엇을 가지고 있지 않다면 그것을 가져가는 과정을(the process of getting it.) 즐길 수 있다.
→ 가진 것이 있다면 가진 것을 즐길 수 있고 가진 것이 없다면 가지려고 하는 그 과정을 즐길 수 있다.

I think life is a type of game.
나는 생각한다. 인생은 게임의 일종이라고
→ 인생은 게임과도 같다고 생각한다.

But what kind of game do you like? Too easy game or Not easy game? Keep this your mind! No pain, no gain. No pain, No pleasures.
그러나 어떤 게임(what kind of game)을 좋아하는가(do you like)? 너무 쉬운 게임? 아니면 쉽지 않은 게임? 명심하시라. 노력하지 않고 얻을 수는 없으며 쉬우면 재미도 없다. (힘들지 않으면 얻는 것이 없고 힘들지 않으면 즐거움도 없다.)

04 As if

As I said, I'm rich now. And my son is rich, too. I think my son doesn't know poverty. But he always talks as if he knew poverty. My son was not poor. But he always talks as if he had been poor for a long time. Mike lives next to my house. He is a friend of my son. He is poor. I think he doesn't know the rich. But he always talks as if he were rich. He was not rich. But he always talks as if he had been rich for a long time.

The poor have their own pains and pleasures. The rich have their own pains and pleasures, too. The poor are worried about money itself. The rich are worried about losing money. All the people have their own pains and pleasures. If you are poor, please don't talk as if you knew the rich. If you are not poor, please don't talk as if you were poor. And... please do not talk as if you knew everything about life.

단어 및 숙어

as [æz] ~처럼(as에는 다양한 기능과 의미가 있으며 접속사 편에서 자세히 다룬다)
itself [it'self] 그 자체
know [nou] / knew [nju:] / known [noun]
lose [lu:z] 잃다, 빼앗기다
own [oun] 자신의 / 소유하다
pain [pein] 고통, 괴로움
pleasure ['pleʒər] 즐거움, 쾌락
poverty ['pa:vərti] 가난, 빈곤

a friend of my son 내 아들의 친구
as if 마치 ~인 것처럼
be worried about ~에 대해 걱정하다
for a long time 오랫동안
lose money 돈을 잃다
next to 바로 옆의, 다음의
pains and pleasures 괴로움과 즐거움
the poor 가난한 사람들/ 가난함
(the 형용사는 ① ~한 사람들 ② 추상명사의 뜻)
the rich 부자들 / 부유함
their own 그들 자신의

해설

① **as if + 가정법 과거** (주어 + 과거동사(be 동사인 경우 were) : 현재 사실의 반대
he always talks as if he knew poverty. 그는 항상 마치 그가 가난을 아는 것처럼 말한다.

② **as if + 가정법 과거완료** (주어 + had 과거분사) : 과거 사실의 반대
he always talks as if he had been poor for a long time.
그는 항상 마치 그가 오랫동안 가난했던 것처럼 말한다.

The poor have their own pains and pleasures.
가난한 사람들은 그들의(가난한 사람들만의) 괴로움과 즐거움이 있다.

The rich are worried about losing money. 부자들은 돈을 잃을까봐 걱정한다.

All the people have their own pains and pleasures.
모든 사람은 그들 자신만의 괴로움과 즐거움이 있다.

If you are poor, please don't talk as if you knew the rich.
만약 당신이 가난하다면 제발 부자들(부유함)을 아는 것처럼 말하지 마세요.

please do not talk as if you knew everything about life.
제발 인생에 관해서 다 아는 것처럼 말하지 마세요.

05 가정법 미래

If I were to be young again, I would try to succeed. But, if I were to be young again, I would not work that hard. If I were to be young again, I would not work that hard just for the money. If I were to be young again, I would try to learn more instead. If I were to be young again, I would try to experience more. If I were to be young again, I would try to love more. If I should be young again, I would try to be happier. If I should be young again, I would try to be wiser. Even if the sun were to rise in the west, I would not change my mind.

I'm rich now, but the same thing happens to me that happens to the poor. I'm getting older and older. I will be dead someday. I have lived earnestly. But what I learned from my life is just three things. What I want to say about life is just three things : Living, loving and learning.

Today could be the last day of your life. When you die, Please don't say, "If I were to....."

단어 및 숙어

change [tʃeindʒ] 바꾸다, 변화하다
dead [ded] 죽은
earnestly [ˈəːnistli] 성실하게, 진지하게
experience [ikˈspiəriəns] 경험하다, 경험
happen [ˈhæpn] 일어나다, 발생하다
instead [inˈsted] ~ 대신에
just [dʒʌst] 단지, 막
mind [maind] 마음, 정신
rise [raiz] 올라오다, 오르다
succeed [səkˈsiːd] 성공하다
west [west] 서쪽
wise [waiz] 현명한, 지혜로운
wiser [wiser] wise(현명한)의 비교급

could be 아마도 어쩌면
even if 설사 ~라 할지라도
get from ~로부터 얻다
get old 늙다, 나이가 들다
get older and older 점점 더 나이가 들다
(get + 비교급 and 비교급 : 점점 더 ~하다)
happen to 일어나다, 발생하다
in the west 서쪽에서
just for the money 단지 돈을 위해서
Living, loving and Learning
삶 사랑 배움, 살며 사랑하며 배우며
that hard 그렇게 힘들게
the last day 마지막 날
the same thing 같은 일

해설

가정법 미래 : 가능성이 낮거나 실현 불가능한 미래의 가정을 나타낸다.
If... should(were to)+ 동사원형..., would(will){should(shall)} + 동사원형

If I were to be young again, I would try to succeed.
만약 다시 젊어진다면 나는 성공을 위해서 노력할 것이다.

If I were to be young again, I would not work that hard just for the money.
만약 다시 젊어진다면, 단지 돈만을 위해서 그렇게 열심히 일하지는 않을 것이다.

If I should be young again, I would try to be happier.
만약 다시 젊어진다면, 더 행복해지려고 노력할 것이다.

But the same thing happens to me that happens to the poor.
그러나 가난한 사람들에게 일어나는 똑같은 일이 나에게도 일어난다.

I'm getting older and older.
나는 점점 더 늙어간다.

But what I learned from my life is just three things.
그러나 내가 인생에서 배운 것(what I learned from my life)은 단지 세 가지이다.

What I want to say about life is just three things.
내가 인생에 관하여 말하고 싶은 것(What I want to say)은 단지 세 가지뿐이다.

Today could be the last day of your life. When you die, Please don't say, "If I were to......"
오늘이 당신 인생의 마지막 날이 될 수도 있습니다. 죽을 때 "만약 내가 .... 한다면"이라고 말하지 마세요.

PART 12.
As

01 부사 역할 as ~ as

I'm Mike. I am 15 years old. I am tall and smart. I have a friend. His name is Tom. He is as old as me. He is as tall as me. And he is as smart as me. His face is as white as snow. I live in a mountain. But the mountain is not as high as you think. I will be waiting for your letter. Please send me a letter as soon as possible.

02 전치사 역할

I want to be your friend. And I came here as a friend. I'm not your enemy. Please don't treat me as an enemy. Please treat me as a friend.

My father works as a doctor. He is famous as a doctor. I don't respect him as a farther. But I respect him as a doctor.

단어 및 숙어

doctor [ˈdaktər] 의사, 박사
enemy [ˈenəmi] 적, 원수
face [feis] 얼굴
famous [ˈfeiməs] 유명한
high [hai] 높은
mountain [ˈmauntin] 산
possible [ˈpasəbl] 가능한

respect [riˈspekt] 존경하다
snow [snou] 눈
treat [tri:t] 다루다, 대우하다
as soon as possible 가능한 빨리

wait for ~을 기다리다

해설

부사 역할

as ~ as : ~만큼 ~한 (동등비교)

He is as old as me. He is as tall as me.
그는 나만큼 나이를 먹었다. 그는 나만큼 키가 크다. → 그는 나와 나이가 같다. 그는 나와 키도 비슷하다.

His face is as white as snow.
그의 얼굴은 눈처럼 희다. (피부가 눈처럼 하얗다.)

But the mountain is not as high as you think.
그러나 그 산은 당신의 생각처럼 높지 않다. → 그러나 그 산은 당신이 생각하는 산처럼 높은 산은 아니다.

전치사 역할 : ~로서

본문의 밑줄을 그은 as는 모두 전치사로서 "~로서"의 의미이다.

I came here as a friend.
나는 친구로서 여기에 왔습니다.

Please don't treat me as an enemy.
나를 원수로 대하지 말아 주세요.

I don't respect him as a farther. But I respect him as a doctor.
나는 아버지로서 존경하지 않지만 의사로서는 존경한다.

03 접속사 역할 ① 시간

I was going to my house. I was happy. I sang a song <u>as</u> I walked along the street. <u>As</u> I arrived at home, my father was leaving the house. <u>As</u> I walked in, I said, "Mom, I'm home." But mom was not in the house. My brother was watching the TV in the living room. I saw that my sister was studying in her room. <u>As</u> she studied, she listened to music.

03 접속사 역할 ② 방법

I asked my sister to buy a cake and some flowers this morning. But there was no cake. She bought some flowers and bread, instead. She did not do <u>as</u> I had asked. I said to my sister, "You didn't do <u>as</u> I asked you. Please do <u>as</u> I told you." She said, "I'm sorry. I will do <u>as</u> you say."

단어 및 숙어

arrive [əˈraiv] 도착하다
bread [bred] 빵
buy [bai] / bought [bɔ:t] / bought [bɔ:t]
instead [inˈsted] 대신에
leave [li:v] 떠나다 / 남기고 가다
music [ˈmju:zik] 음악
sing [siŋ] / sang [sæŋ] / sung [sʌŋ]
song [sɔ:ŋ] 노래

arrive at ~에 도착하다
listen to music 음악을 듣다
listen to 듣다, 경청하다
living room 거실
sing a song 노래를 부르다
walk along the street 길을 걷다, 길을 따라서 걷다
walk in 들어가다, 걸어 들어가다

해설

접속사 역할

① **시간 :** ~ 하자, ~ 하면서, ~할 때에, ~하는 동안

I sang a song as I walked along the street.
길을 걸으면서 노래를 불렀다.

As I arrived at home, my father was leaving the house.
내가 집에 도착했을 때 아버지는 집을 나가고(떠나고) 있었다.

As I walked in, I said, "Mom, I'm home." 걸어 들어가면서 "엄마 저 왔어요."라고 말했다.

② **방법 상태 :** ~처럼 ~한 대로

I asked my sister to buy a cake and some flowers this morning.
오늘 아침 나의 누이에게 케이크와 꽃을 좀 사오라고 부탁하였다.

She did not do as I had asked. 그녀는 내가 부탁한대로 하지 않았다.

You didn't do as I asked you. Please do as I told you.
내가 부탁한대로 하지 않았구나. 제발 내가 말한 대로 해다오.

She said, "I'm sorry. I will do as you say."
"미안해 오빠가 말한 대로 할게."라고 누이는 말했다.

03 접속사 역할 ③ 원인 이유

I go to a university. I also work part time. So I came home late. There was a recorded message. "As you are out, I leave a message. I need your help. Please come to my house as soon as possible." It was Tom. As he always asked for too much, I didn't like him. I called him. "I'm back home now. But it is almost midnight, I can't go there." "Please help me. I just moved here last week. Just one more time. Please...." I thought he might need some help as he just moved to a new house. But It was too late. and I was tired And I had no car.

03 접속사 역할 ④ ~하다시피

I said, "As you know, I have no car. I would like to go there. But I can't." Tom said, "Take a taxi. I will give you money. As you know, my father died a long time ago. As you know, I'm an only child. I have no brothers and sisters. I moved here last week. So I have no friends in this city. There is no one to help me. Please help me. Just one more time. Please...."

As is often the case with him, he never gives up. I remember his father. Tom is tall, as was his father. Tom is fat, as was his father. Tom is lazy, as was his father.

단어 및 숙어

almost [ˈɔːlmoust] 거의
fat [fæt] 살찐
lazy [ˈleizi] 게으른
leave [liːv] / left [left] / left [left] 남기다 / 떠나다
message [ˈmesidʒ] 메시지, 전갈
midnight [ˈmidnait] 자정, 한밤중
move [muːv] 이사하다, 움직이다
possible [ˈpasəbl] 가능한
record [riˈkɔːrd] 기록하다, 녹음하다
remember [riˈmembər] 기억하다

a long time ago 오래전에
As is often the case with ~에 흔히 있는 일이지만
ask for 부탁하다, 필요로 하다
as soon as possible 가능한 빨리
give up 포기하다, 단념하다
Just one more time 딱 한 번만 더
last week 지난주
leave a message 메시지를 남기다
only child 외동아들, 외동딸
recorded message 녹음된 메시지
take a taxi 택시를 타다
would like to ~하고 싶다

해설

③ 원인 이유 : ~때문에 ~이므로

As you are out, I leave a message. 네가 나가고 없어서 메시지를 남긴다.

As he always asked for too much, I didn't like him.
그는 항상 너무 많은 부탁을 하기 때문에 나는 그를 좋아하지 않았다.

④ ~하다시피 ~하듯이

As you know, I have no car. 네가 알다시피 나는 차가 없다.

As you know, my father died a long time ago.
네가 알다시피 나의 아버님은 오래전에 돌아가셨다.

I thought he might need some help as he just moved to a new house.
새집에 막 이사를 왔기 때문에 도움이 필요할 것이라고 생각했다.

As is often the case with him, he never gives up.
그가 흔히 그렇듯이 그는 결코 포기하지 않는다.

Tom is tall, as was his father. Tom is fat, as was his father.
그의 아버지가 그렇듯이 톰은 키가 크다. 그의 아버지가 그렇듯이 톰은 뚱뚱하다.

as was his father. = as his father was의 도치구문이다.

03 접속사 역할 ⑤ ~함에 따라

As we grow older, we become wiser. As we grow older, we become more diligent. But Tom was different. As he grew older, he became more foolish. As he grew older, he became lazier. I really didn't want to go to Tom's house. But he kept asking me for help. Finally, I said, "Okay, I will go."

03 접속사 역할 ⑥ 양보 : ~이지만

I hung up the phone. And I sat on the chair. I remembered my childhood. Smart as I was, I was poor. Poor as I was, I was happy. And I had a dream. But Tom was much different. Rich as he was, he was foolish. Rich as he was, he was lazy. Rich as he was, he always needed my help. Rich as he was, he was not happy.

Poor as my father was, he was diligent. I learned diligence from my father. Tom's father was rich. That's because Tom's grandfather left a great fortune to Tom's father. But Tom's father was lazy. And his father had spent a lot of money. His father couldn't leave a fortune to him. He was rich when he was a child but he isn't now.

단어 및 숙어

chair [tʃeər] 의자
childhood [ˈtʃaildhud] 어린 시절, 유년
different [ˈdifərənt] 다른
diligence [ˈdilidʒəns] 근면, 부지런함
diligent [ˈdilidʒənt] 부지런한, 근면한
Finally [ˈfainəli] 마침내
foolish [ˈfu:liʃ] 어리석은, 바보같은
fortune [ˈfɔ:rtʃu:n] 재산 / 운
grandfather [ˈgrændfaðər] 할아버지
grow [grou] / grew [gru:] / grown [groun]
hang [hæŋ] / hung [hʌŋ] / hung [hʌŋ]
keep [ki:p] / kept [kept] / kept [kept]

lazier 더 게으른(lazy[ˈleizi]의 비교급)
leave [li;v] / left [left] / left [left]
phone [foun] 전화
remember [riˈmembər] 기억하다
sit [sit] / sat [sæt] / sat [sæt]
spend [spend] / spent [spent] / spent [spent]

hang up 전화를 끊다
keep ~ing 계속해서 ~하다
leave a great fortune to
~에게 많은 재산을 물려주다
That's because 그것은 ~ 때문이다

해설

⑤ ~함에 따라

As we grow older, we become wiser. As we grow older, we become more diligent.
우리는 나이가 들어감에 따라 좀 더 현명해진다. 우리는 나이가 들어감에 따라 좀 더 부지런해진다.

But he kept asking me for help. 하지만 그는 계속해서 도움을 요청했다.

⑥ 양보 : ~이지만

Smart as I was, I was poor. Poor as I was, I was happy.
나는 똑똑했지만, 가난했다. 가난했지만, 나는 행복했다.

Rich as he was, he was foolish. Rich as he was, he was lazy.
그는 부자였지만 어리석었다. 그는 부자였지만 게을렀다.

Poor as my father was, he was diligent. 나의 아버지는 가난했지만 부지런하셨다.

That's because Tom's grandfather left a great fortune to Tom's father.
그것은 탐의 할아버지가 탐의 아버지에게 많은 재산을 물려주었기 때문이다.

He was rich when he was a child but he isn't now.
탐은 어렸을 때는 부자였지만 지금은 아니다.

His father had spent a lot of money before he died. When his father was alive Tom spent a lot of money, too. And Tom has spent all the money that he got from his father.

I had left my hometown and came here. I had left my home town and came here to go to Harvard University. I got a scholarship. Poor as I am, I have a dream. Poor as I am, I have a vision. Tom had left his hometown.... and came here... to be a waiter. I think he has no dream.

Every life has its ups and downs. Not every man <u>is born with a silver spoon in his mouth</u>. However, bad luck sometimes brings good luck. And good luck sometimes brings bad luck, too. The poor can be rich and the rich can be poor. That is the way life goes.

Do you want to know about your life? If you want to know your past, watch what you are receiving now. If you want to know your future, watch what you are doing now. Your life is what you have been making and what you are making now. Nobody can make you happy. Nobody can make you rich. Nobody can change your life except you. Nobody can decide your life except you. Create your own future!

단어 및 숙어

Create [kriˈeit] 창조하다
decide [diˈsaid] 결정하다, 결심하다
except [ikˈsept] ~을 제외하고
fortune [ˈfɔːrtʃuːn] 재산 / 운
hometown [ˈhoumtaun] 고향
leave [liːv] 남기다 / 떠나다
luck [lʌk] 운, 운명
mouth [mauθ] 입
past [pæst] 과거, 지나간
receive [riˈsiːv] 받다
scholarship [ˈskalərʃip] 장학금
silver [ˈsilvər] 은
spend [spend] / spent [spent] / spent [spent]
spoon [spuːn] 수저
university [juːniˈvərsəti] 대학교
vision [ˈviʒən] 비젼, 시야
waiter [ˈweitər] 웨이터, 급사

bad luck 불운
be born with a silver spoon in one's mouth 은수저를 물고 태어나다.
get from ~로부터 받다
good luck 행운
Harvard university 하버드대학
leave a great fortune to ~에게 많은 재산을 물려주다
silver spoon 은수저, 상속받은 재산
ups and downs 오르막과 내리막, 우여곡절, 흥망성쇠

해설

Tom has spent all the money that he got from his father.
탐은 그의 아버지로부터 받은 (that he got from his father) 모든 재산을 다 써버렸다.

I had left my home town and came here to go to Harvard university.
나는 하버드 대학에 다니기 위하여 고향을 떠나 여기에 왔다.

Poor as I am, I have a dream. Poor as I am, I have a vision.
나는 가난하지만 꿈이 있고 가난하지만 비전이 있다.

Every life has its ups and downs.
인생에는 오르막이 있고 내리막이 있다.

Not every man is born with a silver spoon in his mouth.
모든 사람이 은수저를(with a silver spoon) 물고(in his mouth) 태어나지 않는다.
(서양 속담) → 모든 사람이 부자로 태어나지 않는다.

sometimes bad luck brings good luck and good luck sometimes brings bad luck.
가끔은 불행이 행운을 가져오기도 하고 행운이 불행을 가져 오기도 한다.

That is the way life goes.
그것이 인생(life)이 가는(goes) 길(the way)이다. → 인생이란 그런 것이다.

If you want to know your past, watch what you are receiving now.
만약 당신의 과거를 알고 싶다면 지금 당신이 받고 있는 것(what you are receiving now)을 보아라.
→ 지금 현재의 당신은 당신의 과거가 만든 것이다.

Your life is what you made and what you are making now.
당신의 인생은 당신이 만들었던 것(what you made)과 당신이 지금 만들고 있는 것(what you are making now)이다.

Nobody can decide your life except you.
당신을 빼고 누구도 당신의 인생을 결정할 수는 없다.

PART 13.
관계대명사

01 Who ① 주격

(01)

Mike is a teacher. He came from New York. He has a sister. His sister plays the piano well. His sister is really pretty.

Mike is a teacher who came from New York. He has a sister who plays the piano well. He has a sister who is really pretty.

(02)

"Do you know the tall man? He is reading a book."
"Yes, I know the tall man. He likes to play baseball. The man is a cop. He is working at the police station. He is terrible."
"Terrible? What do you mean?"
"I mean he is cruel."
"Cruel? Wow! He is really terrible."

"Do you know the tall man who is reading a book?"
"Yes, I know the tall man who likes to play baseball. The tall man who is reading a book is terrible. The tall man who is working at the police station is a cop."

단어 및 숙어

baseball [ˈbeisbɔːl] 야구
cop [kaːp] 경찰
cruel [ˈkruːəl] 잔인한
mean [miːn] 의미하다, –할 작정이다
police [pəˈliːs] 경찰
pretty [ˈpriti] 예쁜, 아름다운

station [ˈsteiʃən] 역
terrible [ˈterəbl] 끔찍한, 무시무시한
wow [wau] 와(감탄사)

police station 경찰서

해설

관계대명사
관계대명사는 앞에 나오는 명사나 대명사를 대신해 주는 대명사의 역할과 뒤에 나오는 절을 결합시켜 주는 접속사 역할을 한다.

선행사
관계대명사가 대신 받는 말 일반적으로 관계사 앞에 위치하는 명사나 명사구를 가리킨다.

Mike is a teacher who came from New York. (teacher가 선행사이다.)

Who : 선행사가 사람일 때 일반적으로 쓰인다.

① 주격

Mike is a teacher who came from New York.
마이크는 뉴욕에서 온 선생님(a teacher who came from New York)이다.

He has a sister who plays the piano well.
그는 피아노를 잘 치는 여동생(a sister who plays the piano well)이 있다.

Do you know the tall man who is reading a book?
책을 읽고 있는 키가 큰 사람(the man who is reading a book)을 아십니까?

The tall man who is reading a book is terrible.
책을 읽고 있는 키가 큰 사람(The man who is reading a book)은 무서운 사람이다.

01 Who ② whose

"Do you know that man? His bag is green."
"Who?"
"I mean that handsome guy. His dog is white."
"Yes, I know that man. His name is Tom. His father is a teacher."

"Do you know that man whose bag is green?"
"Who?'
"I mean that handsome guy whose dog is white."
"Yes, I know that man whose name is Tom. I know that man whose father is a teacher."

01 Who ③ whom (who)

"Mom, he is the man."
"What do you mean?"
"I met him yesterday. I met him in the park."
"I see."
"Mom, she is the woman."
"What do you mean?"
"I saw her in the morning. I saw her in the street."
"I see."

단어 및 숙어

green [gri:n] 녹색
guy [gai] 남자, 사람
handsome [ˈhænsəm] 잘 생긴
mean [mi:n] 의미하다
meet [mi:t] / met [met] / met [met]
만나다

that [ðæt] 저, 그
whom [hu:m] 누구를
whose [hu:z] 누구의

I see 알겠다, 그렇군
that man 저 사람

해설

② 소유격 whose

Do you know that man whose bag is green?
그의 가방(whose bag)이 녹색인 저 사람을 아십니까?

I know that man whose father is a teacher.
그의 아버지(whose father)가 선생님인 그 사람을 압니다.

③ 목적격 whom

구어체에서는 whom 대신에 who를 더 많이 쓴다.

"Mom, he is the man whom I met yesterday."
"I see."
"Mom, he is the man whom I met in the park."
"I see....."
"Mom, she is the woman whom I saw in the morning."
"I see... Please... stop it."
"Mom, she is the woman whom I met in the street."
"I see. stop it!"

02 Which ① 일반적인 용법

Look at that nice pen. It is on the table. I will have that pen.
This is the pen. It was made in France.

Look at the nice pen which is on the table. I will have the pen which is on the table.

That is the pen which was made in France. The pen which is on the table was made in France.

단어 및 숙어

meet [miːt] / met [met] / met [met]
France [fræns] 프랑스
whom [huːm] 누구를
whose [huːz] 누구의

be made in ～에서 만들어지다
I see 알겠다, 그렇군
stop it 멈춰라, 그만해라

해설

③ 목적격 whom
구어체에서는 whom 대신에 who를 더 많이 쓴다.

Mom he is the man whom I met yesterday. = Mom he is the man who I met yesterday.
(구어체) 엄마 저 분이 내가 어제 만났던 사람이에요.

Mom she is the woman whom I saw in the morning.
= Mom she is the woman who I saw in the morning.
(구어체) 엄마 저 분은 아침에 내가 보았던 여자 분이에요.

I see…. Please… stop it ! 알겠다. 제발… 그만해라!

Which

① 일반적 용법
동물이나 사물 사건 등을 수식할 때와 앞 문장 전체를 받을 때 주로 쓴다.

Look at that nice pen which is on the table.
탁자 위에 있는(which is on the table) 멋진 펜을 보세요.

That is the pen which was made in France.
저것은 프랑스에서 만들어진(which was made in France) 펜이다.

The pen which is on the table was made in France.
탁자 위에 있는(which is on the table) 펜은 프랑스에서 만들어진 펜이다.

02 Which ② 앞 문장 전체를 받는 which

My sister came home late last night. It was unusual. My father waited for her until midnight. It made him angry. My sister drank a lot. It made him angrier.

My sister came home late last night, which was unusual. My father waited for her until midnight, which made him angry. My sister drank a lot, which made him angrier.

03 That

I like this pen. Mike gave it to me.
I like this pen that Mike gave to me.

Look at the girl. And look at her dog. They are running.
Look at the girl and her dog that are running.

I am looking at the handsome man. Do you know the handsome man?
Do you know the handsome man that I am looking at?

단어 및 숙어

angrier [ˈæŋgriər] 더 화난, angry의 비교급
drink [driŋk] / drank [dræŋk] / drunk [drʌŋk]
give [giv] / gave [geiv] / given [givn]
late [leit] 늦은, 늦게

midnight [ˈmidnait] 자정, 한밤중
till [til] ~까지
unusual [ʌnˈjuːʒuəl] 드문, 흔치 않은

look at ~을 보다

해설

② 앞 문장 전체를 받는 which

My sister came home late last night, which was unusual.
나의 여동생은 어젯밤에 집에 늦게 왔는데 그것은(which) 드문 일이었다.
여기서 which는 앞 문장 전체의 내용을 가리킨다.

My father waited for her until midnight, which made him angry.
나의 아버지는 자정까지 그녀를 기다렸는데 그것이(which) 아버지를 화나게 하였다.

That

선행사가 사람, 동물, 사물인지에 관계없이 모든 경우에 사용한다.
① 선행사가 사람+동물, 사람+사물, 선행사 앞의 형용사가 the only, the very, all 등이 쓰인 경우에는 주로 that을 사용한다.
② 선행사가 사람인 경우 구어체에서는 that보다는 who를 주로 사용한다.

I like this pen that Mike gave to me.
나는 마이크가 내게 준 이 펜을 좋아한다.

Look at the girl and her dog that are running.
달리고 있는 저 소녀와 그녀의 개를 보아라.

I know Tom. Tom is playing baseball. He is wearing a blue shirt. His uncle bought it for him.

I know Tom that is playing baseball. He is wearing a blue shirt that his uncle bought for him.

04 What

We must do what is right. We must see what is beautiful. We must think what is good. What we want to see are beautiful things. What we want to think are good things.

You are special. You are very special. You are not what you think you are. You are more than what you think you are. Do not follow too much of what other people do. Do not believe too much of what other people say.

You can achieve what you imagine. If you are not lazy, you can achieve what you want. If you are diligent, you can get what you need. But if you are lazy, forget what I told you. If you are lazy, you will not achieve anything in the future.

단어 및 숙어

achieve [əˈtʃiːv] 달성하다, 성취하다
believe [biˈliːv] 믿다
blue [bluː] 푸른
buy [bai] / bought [bɔːt] / bought [bɔːt]
diligent [ˈdilidʒənt] 근면한, 부지런한
follow [ˈfaːlou] 따르다, 쫓다
forget [fərˈget] 잊다
future [ˈfjuːtʃər] 미래
imagine [iˈmædʒin] 상상하다
lazy [ˈleizi] 게으른

other [ˈʌðər] 다른, 다른 사람
right [rait] 올바른, 알맞는
shirt [ʃəːrt] 셔츠
special [ˈspeʃəl] 특별한
uncle [ˈʌŋkl] 삼촌, 아저씨
wear [weər] 입다

해설

I know Tom that is playing baseball.
나는 야구를 하고 있는 (that is playing baseball) 톰을 안다.

He is wearing a blue shirt that his uncle bought for him.
그 소년은 그의 삼촌이 자기에게 사준 (that his uncle bought for him) 푸른 셔츠를 입고 있다.

What

관계대명사 what은 선행사를 포함하고 있으며 '~하는 것'으로 해석하면 무난하다. 관계대명사 what은 that which, those which, the thing which, all that 등으로 바꾸어 쓸 수 있다.

We must do what is right.
우리는 옳은 일(what is right.)을 하여야 한다.

What we want to see are beautiful things.
우리가 보기를 원하는 것(What we want to see)은 아름다운 것들이다.

You are not what you think you are.
당신은 당신이 생각하는(what you think) 당신은 ~한 존재다(you are)가 아니다.
→ 당신은 당신이 생각하는 그런 존재(what you think you are)가 아니다.

You are more than what you think you are.
당신은 당신이 생각하는(what you think) 당신은 ~한 사람이다(you are.) 보다 더 나은(more than) 사람이다.
→ 당신은 당신이 생각하는 그런 사람(what you think you are)보다 더 나은 존재이다.

Do not follow too much of what other people do.
다른 사람이 하는 것(what other people do)을 너무 따라 하지 마라.
→ 다른 사람이 하는 행동을 너무 따라 하려 하지 마라.

You can achieve what you imagine.
당신은 당신이 상상하는 것(what you imagine)을 이룰 수 있다.
→ 당신이 상상할 수 있는 (모든 것을) 이룰 수 있다.

If you are not lazy, you can achieve what you want.
만약 당신이 게으르지 않다면, 당신은 당신이 원하는 것(what you want)은 (어떤 것도) 이룰 수가 있다.

But if you are lazy, forget what I told you.
그러나 만약 당신이 게으르다면, 내가 당신에게 말한 것(what I told you)을 잊어버려라.
→ 그러나 만약 당신이 게으르다면, 내가 한 말은 잊어버려라.

Do you want to know about your life? If you want to know your past, watch what you are receiving now. If you want to know your future, watch what you are making now. Your life is what you have made and what you are making now. Nobody can decide your life except you.

Remember you are the only one who can call yourself, "I". Nobody can call you, "I" throughout the whole universe except yourself. Even God can not call you, "I". You are "the One" that Neo['ni:ou]* said.

* Neo['ni:ou] 매트릭스란 영화의 주인공

단어 및 숙어

except [ikˈsept] ~을 제외하고
future [ˈfjuːtʃər] 미래
past [pæst] 과거, 지나간
receive [riˈsiːv] 받다
throughout [θruːˈaut] ~에 걸쳐서, 도처에

universe [ˈjuːnivəːrs] 우주
whole [houl] 전체의
Neo [ˈniːou] 매트릭스란 영화의 주인공

the only one 유일한 존재

해설

If you want to know your past, watch what you are receiving now.
만약 당신의 과거를 알고 싶다면 지금 당신이 받고 있는 것(what you are receiving now)을 보아라.
→ 지금 현재의 당신은 당신의 과거가 만든 것이다.

Your life is what you have made and what you are making now.
당신의 인생은 당신이 만들어 왔던 것(what you have made)과 당신이 지금 만들고 있는 것 (what you are making now)이다.

Nobody can decide your life except you.
당신을 제외하고(except you) 그 누구도 당신의 인생을 결정할 수는 없다.

you are the only one who can call yourself, "I".
당신은 당신을 "나"라고 부를 수 있는 (who can call yourself, "I".) 유일한 존재이다.

Nobody can call you, "I" throughout the whole universe except yourself.
우주 전체를 통하여(throughout the whole universe) 당신을 "나"라고 부를 수 있는 (can call you, "I") 사람은 당신을 제외하고는(except yourself) 아무도 없다.

You are 'the One' that Neo[ˈniːou] said.
당신은 니오(매트릭스라는 영화의 주인공)가 말한 바로 그 "the One"이다.

PART 14.
조동사

01 must have + 과거분사

(01)

"Did you see her husband?" "No, I didn't see her husband yet.[1] Why did you ask?" "I was surprised to see him. He is tall and handsome. He also looks smart. He must have graduated from college.[2] I wonder why he married her." "He must have married her for the money.[3] Her father is very rich. Didn't you know that? "Yes, I did. I knew it."

(02)

He came back home late last night.[4] And he got up late this morning. He must have had too much drink last night.[5] I knew he had no money to drink. Then, how did he drink? My husband must have given him some money.[6]

(03)

She is not young. She is not healthy. Her health is not good. She is sick in bed.[7] Her face is as white as snow.[8] Her eyes are as blue as the sea.[9] The doctor can feel her beauty. She must have been beautiful when she was healthy.[10]

해설

must have + 과거분사
~했음에 틀림없다. (분명히) ~ 했었을 것이다. : 과거 사실에 대한 강한 추측을 나타낸다.

1) No, I didn't see her husband yet. 아니오, 나는 아직 그녀의 남편을 보지 않았어요.
2) He must have graduated from college. 그는 틀림없이 대학을 졸업했을 거예요.

단어 및 숙어

beauty ['bju:ti] 아름다움
blue [blu:] 파란, 푸른
college ['ka:lidʒ] 대학
come [kʌm] / came [keim] / come [kʌm] 오다
doctor ['da:ktər] 의사, 박사
face [feis] 얼굴
feel [fi:l] 느끼다
get [get] / got [gat] / got [gat], gotten [gatn]
give [giv] / gave [geiv] / given [givn] 주다
graduate [동) 'grædʒueit 명) 'grædʒuit] 졸업하다, 졸업
handsome ['hænsəm] 잘 생긴
have [hæv] / had [hæd] / had [hæd] 마시다, 먹다 / 가지다
health [helθ] 건강
healthy ['helθi] 건강한
husband ['hʌzbənd] 남편
know [nou] / knew [nju:] / known [noun] 알다

last [last] 지난
late [leit] 늦은
marry ['mæri] ~와 결혼하다
money ['mʌni] 돈
must [mʌst] ~해야 한다
smart [sma:rt] 똑똑한, 영리한
surprise [sər'praiz] 놀라게 하다
wonder ['wʌndər] 궁금하다
yet [jet] 아직

as … as ~ ~만큼 …한
as blue as the sea 바다만큼 푸른
as white as snow 눈처럼 하얀
be surprised 놀라다
come back 돌아오다
get up 일어나다
get up late 늦게 일어나다
have too much drink 과음하다, 술을 많이 마시다

3) He must have married her for the money. 그는 (분명히) 돈 때문에 그녀와 결혼 했을 거예요.
4) He came back home late last night. 그는 어제 늦게 집에 돌아왔다.
5) He must have had too much drink last night. 그는 어젯밤에 과음을 했음에 틀림이 없다.
6) My husband must have given him some money. 내 남편이 분명히 그에게 돈을 주었을 것이다.
7) She is sick in bed. 그녀는 아파서 누워있다.
8) Her face is as white as snow. 그녀의 얼굴은 눈처럼 희다.
9) Her eyes are as blue as the sea. 그녀의 눈은 바다처럼 푸르다.
10) She must have been beautiful when she was healthy. 그녀가 건강했을 때는 분명히 아름다웠을 것이다.

02 should have + 과거분사

(01)
"There are too many cars on the street. We are going to be late again.¹⁾ We should have taken a shortcut.²⁾ I told you to take a shortcut. Do you remember? I suggested taking a shortcut. You should have followed my advice. I told you to tell the taxi driver to take a shortcut.³⁾

But you didn't tell him to go the way that I suggested. Why didn't you tell him to go the way that I suggested?⁴⁾ You should have told the taxi driver to go that way. You should have told the taxi driver to go the way that I suggested."⁵⁾ "Stop it! I can't stand it any more. Stop it! You should have gotten up earlier. If you had gotten up earlier, this would not have happened.⁶⁾ And you should have gone to bed earlier."⁷⁾

(02)
Two kids were killed. Their mother was sleeping in the car. She didn't know that her children had gotten out of the car.⁸⁾ She should have watched the children more carefully.⁹⁾ Or, at least she should have locked the door of the car.¹⁰⁾

단어 및 숙어

advice [əd'vais] 조언, 충고
carefully ['keərfəli] 신중하게, 주의깊게
children ['tʃildrən] 아이들
driver ['draivər] 운전자
follow ['fa:lou] 따르다
last [last] 지난
late [leit] 늦은
least : [li:st] 가장 적은
little ['litl] < less [les] < least [li:st]
lock [la:k] 잠그다
remember [ri'membər] 기억하다
shortcut ['ʃɔ:rtkʌt] 지름길
sleep [sli:p] / slept [slept] / slept [slept] 잠자다
stand [stænd] 참다, 견디다 / 서다

street [stri:t] 거리
suggest [sə'dʒest] 제안하다
taxi ['tæksi] 택시
tell [tel] / told [tould] / told [tould] 말하다
watch [wa:tʃ] 보다

any more 더 이상
at least 적어도
get out of ~ ~에서 나오다
I can stand it any more 더 이상 못 참겠다
suggest ~ing ~할 것을 제안하다
take a shortcut 지름길로 가다

해설

should have + 과거분사

~했어야 했는데 (하지 못했다.) : 과거에 있었던 일에 대한 후회나 원망을 나타낸다.

1) We are going to be late again. 우리 또 늦겠다.
2) We should have taken a shortcut. 우리는 지름길로 갔어야만 했다.
3) I told you to tell the taxi driver to take a shortcut.
택시 운전사에게 지름길로 가자고 말해야 한다고 너에게 말했잖아.
4) Why didn't you tell him to go the way that I suggested?
왜 너는 내가 제안한 길로 가자고 그에게 말하지 않았니?
5) You should have told the taxi driver to go the way that I suggested.
너는 내가 제안한 길로 가자고 택시 운전사에게 말했어야만 했다.
6) If you had gotten up earlier, this would not have happened.
만약 네가 조금 더 일찍 일어났다면 이런 일은 일어나지 않았을 거야.
7) And you should have gone to bed earlier. 그리고 너는 좀 더 일찍 잠들었어야 했어.
8) She didn't know that her children had gotten out of the car.
그녀는 그녀의 아이들이 차에서 나간 것을 알지 못했다.
9) She should have watched the children more carefully. 그녀는 그 아이들을 주의 깊게 살펴보아야만 했었다.
10) Or, at least she should have locked the door of the car. 아니면 그녀는 최소한 차의 문을 잠겼어야 했다.

03 may have + 과거분사

(01)

I went to his room. He wasn't in his room. I went to the garage. I couldn't find his car in the garage. He might have left last night.[1] If he had left last night, he might have already arrived at his home.[2]

(02)

I tried to find my wallet. But I couldn't find my wallet. I might have left it at the restaurant.[3]

(03)

I did everything to find the file. But the file was not to be found.[4] It might have been deleted.[5] I was worried that I might have made a mistake.[6]

(04)

He usually doesn't make any mistakes. But, he always worries too much about everything. He didn't make any mistakes in his work yesterday. But he is worried that he might have made a mistake in his work.[7]

단어 및 숙어

already [ɔːlˈredi] 이미, 벌써
arrive [əˈraiv] 도착하다
delete [diˈliːt] 삭제하다
everything [ˈevriθiŋ] 모든 것
file [fail] 파일, 서류철
find [faind] / found [faund] / found [faund] 발견하다
garage [gəˈraːʤ] 차고
go [gou] / went [went] / gone [gɔːn] 가다
last [last] 지난
leave [liːv] / left [left] / left [left] 떠나다
make [meik] / made [meid] / made [meid] 만들다

may [mei] ~일지도 모른다
mistake [miˈsteik] 실수
restaurant [ˈrestəraːnt] 식당
try [trai] 노력하다
usually [ˈjuːʒuəli] 보통, 대개
wallet [ˈwaːlit] 지갑
work [wəːrk] 직장 / 일, 일하다
worry [ˈwəːri] 걱정하다, 근심하다

go to ~ ~에 가다
make a mistake 실수하다
try to ~ ~하려고 노력하다

해설

may(might) have + 과거분사

~ 했을지도 모른다. 아마도 ~했었을 것이다. : 과거에 있었던 일에 대한 약한 추측을 나타낸다.

1) He might have left last night. 그는 아마도 지난밤에 떠났을 것이다.
2) If he had left last night, he might have already arrived at his home.
만약 그가 지난밤에 떠났다면, 이미 그의 집에 도착했을 것이다.
3) I might have left it at the restaurant. 어쩌면 식당에 놓고 왔을지도 모른다.
4) But the file was not to be found. 그러나 파일은 발견되지 않았다.
5) It might have been deleted. 그 파일은 삭제되었는지도 모른다.
6) I was worried that I might have made a mistake. 내가 실수를 했을까봐 걱정했다.
7) But he is worried that he might have made a mistake in his work.
그러나 그가 일에 실수를 했을까봐 걱정한다.

04 Can not help ~ing

My father died when I was a child. My mother died two years ago. And my dog died yesterday. I'm so lonely now. I'm so sad. I cannot help crying.[1)]

He is tall and handsome. He is so kind and gentle. Also He is very smart. I cannot help falling in love with him.[2)]

I can't understand the matter. And I can't believe what Tom told me. So I cannot help asking you about the matter.[3)]

I have a large family to support.[4)] I have to support my family. So I can't help working all day long.[5)]

He is very nice and handsome. He is very kind and gentle. His smile is so sweet and soft.[6)] So I can't help smiling whenever I see him.[7)]

I'm working all day long. I'm hungry all day long. So I can't help eating so much.[8)]

단어 및 숙어

cry [krai] 울다
fall [fɔ:l] 떨어지다 / 가을
gentle ['dʒentl] 다정한, 온화한
handsome ['hænsəm] 잘 생긴
hungry ['hʌŋgri] 배고픈
kind [kaind] 친절한 / 종류
large [la:rdʒ] 큰, 넓은
lonely ['lounli] 외로운
matter ['mætər] 문제
smart [sma:rt] 똑똑한, 영리한
support [sə'pɔ:rt] 부양하다 / 지지하다
sweet [swi:t] 달콤한, 단

tell [tel] / told [tould] / told [tould] 말하다
understand [ʌndər'stænd] 이해하다
whenever [wen'evər] ~할 때마다
year ['jiər] 연도, 1년

all day long 온종일
all the time 항상, 늘
fall in love with ~ ~와 사랑에 빠지다
have to ~해야만 한다

해설

Can not help ~ing
~하지 않을 수 없다.

1) I cannot help crying. 나는 울지 않을 수 없다.
2) I cannot help falling in love with him. 나는 그와 사랑에 빠지지 않을 수 없다.
3) So I cannot help asking you about the matter. 그래서 나는 그 문제에 관하여 너에게 물어보지 않을 수 없다.
4) I have a large family to support. 나는 부양해야 할 가족이 많다.
5) So I can't help working all day long. 그래서 나는 하루 종일 일하지 않을 수 없다.
6) His smile is so sweet and soft. 그의 미소는 정말 부드럽고 감미롭다.
7) So I can't help smiling whenever I see him. 그래서 그를 보면 나는 미소 짓지 않을 수 없다.
8) So I can't help eating so much. 그래서 나는 그렇게 많이 먹지 않을 수 없다.

종합 이해

"She should have been home by now.[1] But she didn't come yet. What happened to her?[2] Something must have happened to her.[3] Or, an accident must have happened to her. I called her office. But nobody answered the phone. I should have called her office earlier."[4] "Honey! please stop worrying about her. She might have just missed the train.[5] And maybe she is waiting for another train." "I see. But I cannot help worrying about what might have happened to her."[6]

단어 및 숙어

accident ['æksidənt] 사고
call [kɔ:l] 전화하다
honey ['hʌni] 여보, 자기 / 벌꿀
maybe ['meibi] 아마, 어쩌면
miss [mis] 놓치다 / 그리워하다
must [mʌst] ~해야 한다
nobody ['noubɑ:di] 아무도 ~않다
office ['ɔ:fis] 사무실
something ['sʌmθiŋ] 어떤 것, 무엇
train [trein] 기차
wait [weit] 기다리다

worry ['wə:ri] 걱정하다, 근심하다
yet [jet] 아직

by now 지금쯤
cannot help worrying
걱정할 수밖에 없다
happen to ~ ~에게 일어나다, 발생하다
stop ~ing ~하는 것을 멈추다
stop worrying 걱정하는 것을 멈추다
wait for ~ ~를 기다리다
worry about ~ ~에 대해 걱정하다

해설

1) She should have been home by now. 그녀는 지금쯤이면 집에 와 있어야 한다.
2) What happened to her? 그녀에게 무슨 일이 생긴 것일까?
3) Something must have happened to her. 그녀에게 필시 무슨 일이 생긴 것이 틀림없다.
4) I should have called her office earlier. 그녀의 사무실로 좀 더 일찍 전화를 했어야 했는데.
5) She might have just missed the train. 그녀는 단지 기차를 놓쳤을 뿐인지도 모른다.
6) But I cannot help worrying about what might have happened to her.
그러나 그녀에게 무슨 일이 생긴 것은 아닐까 걱정하지 않을 수가 없다. (걱정을 멈출 수가 없다.)

PART 15.
5형식 연습

(01)

I need a cup of water. I need a piece of bread. I need a glass of milk. I need a bottle of wine. I need clothes. And I need a piece of advice.

As I told you, what I needed was a cup of water.[1] What I needed was a piece of bread.[2] What I needed was food. What I needed was a house. What I needed were clothes. But those are not all that I need.[3] Above all, I really need the meaning of life. What is the meaning of life? Can you tell me about the meaning of life? Can you? If you can, give me a piece of advice. I need a piece of advice.

(02)

I came here. I came here to see something.[4] I came here to see if you like it or not.[5] I was not sure if you liked it or not.[6] And I came here to know something. I came here to know if the news was true or not.[7] I mean, the news about the accident. I know that you heard something about the accident. Don't tell me a lie. I came here to find out something.[8] I came here to find out if Tom told me the truth or not.[9]

단어 및 숙어

accident ['æksidənt] 사건, 사고
advice [əd'vais] 조언, 충고
bottle ['ba:tl] 병
bread [bred] 빵
clothes [klouz] 옷(복수 명사)
find [faind] 찾다, 발견하다
glass [glæs] 유리잔 / 유리
lie [lai] 거짓말, 거짓말하다
life [laif] 삶, 인생
mean [mi:n] 의미하다
meaning ['mi:niŋ] 의미, 뜻
milk [milk] 우유
news [nju:z] 소식, 뉴스
piece [pi:s] 조각, 한 개
something ['sʌmθiŋ] 어떤 것, 무엇

sure [ʃuər] 확신하는, 확실한
those [ðouz] 저것들(that의 복수형)
wine [wain] 와인, 포도주

a bottle of wine 와인 한 병
a cup of water 한 잔의 물
a glass of milk 한 잔의 우유
a piece of advice 충고 한 마디
a piece of bread 빵 한 조각
above all 무엇보다도
find out 발견하다, 알아내다
see if ~ ~인지 아닌지 알다, ~인지 아닌지 확인하다
tell a lie 거짓말하다
the meaning of life 인생의 의미

해설

1) As I told you, what I needed was a cup of water. 내가 말한 바와 같이, 내가 필요했던 것은 물 한 컵이었다.
2) What I needed was a piece of bread. 내가 필요했던 것은 빵 한 조각이었다.
3) But those are not all that I need. 그러나 그것들이 내가 필요한 전부는 아니다.
4) I came here to see something. 무엇인가를 보기 위해서 여기에 왔다.
5) I came here to see if you like it or not. 네가 그것을 좋아하는지 아닌지 보기 위해서 여기에 왔다.
6) I was not sure if you liked it or not. 나는 네가 그것을 좋아하는지 아닌지 확신할 수 없었다.
7) I came here to know if the news was true or not.
나는 그 소식들이 사실인지 아닌지 알기 위해서 여기에 왔다.
8) I came here to find out something. 나는 무엇인가를 알아내기 위해서 여기에 왔다.
9) I came here to find out if Tom told me the truth or not.
나는 탐이 나에게 사실을 이야기한 것인지 아닌지 알아내기 위해서 여기에 왔다.

(03)

I know you are a good student. But your actions make me angry. And your words make me sad.[1] Please don't act like that.[2] Please don't talk like that. I know your dream is to become a teacher. I know you are an excellent student. You will make an excellent teacher.[3] And I believe you will make an excellent teacher.[4] And I believe you will make a good father someday.[5] Do you understand what I mean? O.K good! From now on, I hope you will become a good boy.[6]

(04)

I have a lot of things to do.[7] Please help me. Bring a pen to me. Bring a pencil to me. I will give some money to you. I will give a letter to you. And I will give your sister's address to you. Send that letter to her. Do you remember what I said?[8] No?

You didn't listen to me carefully. I will say again. Listen to me carefully this time. First, bring me a pen and bring me a pencil.[9] Second, I will give you some money. I will give you a letter. And I will give you your sister's address.[10] Send her that letter. Do you remember what I said? Yes? Okay. Then, do it right now what I told you.[11]

단어 및 숙어

act [ækt] 행동하다
action ['ækʃən] 행동
address ['ædres] 주소
believe [bi'li:v] 믿다
bring [briŋ] 가져오다
carefully ['keərfəli] 신중하게, 주의 깊게
dream [dri:m] 꿈
excellent ['eksələnt] 훌륭한, 우수한
first ['fə:rst] 첫째, 처음의
hope [houp] 바라다, 희망하다
listen ['lisn] 듣다
make [meɪk] (성장하거나 발달하여)
~이 되다 / 만들다
mean [mi:n] 의미하다

money ['mʌni] 돈
second ['sekənd] 두 번째의, 제2의
send [send] 보내다
thing [θiŋ] 것(사물을 가리킴)
understand [ˌʌndər'stænd] 이해하다
word [wə:rd] 말 / 단어

a lot of ~ 많은 ~
from now on 지금부터, 앞으로
like that 그런 식으로, 그렇게
listen to ~ ~을 듣다
right now 지금 당장
this time 이번에는

해설

* **make**는 일반적으로 '~을 만들다', '~이 되게하다'라는 의미로 쓰이지만 '(성장하거나 발전하여) ~이 되다'는 의미로도 사용된다.

1) And your words make me sad. 그리고 너의 말들이 나를 슬프게 한다.
2) Please don't act like that. 제발 그렇게 행동하지 마라.
3) You will make an excellent teacher. 너는 훌륭한 선생님이 될 것이다.
4) And I believe you will make an excellent teacher. 그리고 네가 훌륭한 선생님이 될 것이라고 나는 믿는다.
5) And I believe you will make a good father someday.
그리고 언젠가는 네가 훌륭한 아버지가 될 것이라고 나는 믿는다.
6) From now on, I hope you will become a good boy. 이제부터 나는 네가 착한 소년이 되기를 바란다.
7) I have a lot of things to do. 나는 할 일이 많다.
8) Do you remember what I said? 내가 한 말을 기억하니?
9) First, bring me a pen and bring me a pencil. 첫째 나에게 펜을 갖다 주렴 그리고 연필을 갖다 주렴.
10) And I will give you your sister's address. 그리고 너에게 너의 누이의 주소를 주겠다.
11) Then, do it right now what I told you. 그러면 내가 너에게 말한 것을 즉시 하렴.

(05)

I love Mary. So I bought some flowers for Mary.[1] I love my parents. So I bought some gifts for my parents. I love my brother. So I bought a toy car for my brother. I love my sister. So I bought a pretty doll for my sister.

Do you remember what I did?[2] No? Okay. I will say it again. Listen carefully this time. I bought Mary some flowers. I bought my parents some gifts. I bought my brother a toy car. I bought my sister a pretty doll. That's because I love them.[3] Do you remember what I did? Yes? Good!

(06)

Yesterday, I had a lot of things to do. So I was really busy. My computer did not work well.[4] So I had my computer fixed.[5] My room was dirty. So I had my room cleaned.[6] My shoes were dirty. So I had my shoes shined.[7] My car was dirty. So I had my car washed.[8] I had my bike stolen.[9] So I had to find my bike all afternoon. At last, I found my bike. But the bike had a problem. So I had the bike fixed.[10] And I found that my hair was too long. So I had my hair cut. I had my hair cut short.[11] See! I was really busy yesterday.

단어 및 숙어

again [əˈgen] 또, 다시
bike [baik] 오토바이
buy [bai] / bought [bɔːt] / bought [bɔːt] 사다
carefully [ˈkeərfəli] 신중하게, 주의 깊게
clean [kliːn] 청소하다/깨끗한
computer [kəmˈpjuːtər] 컴퓨터
cut [kʌt] 자르다
dirty [ˈdəːrti] 더러운
doll [daːl] 인형
find [faind] 찾다, 발견하다
find [faind] / found [faund] / found [faund] 발견하다
fix [fiks] 수리하다, 고정시키다
flower [ˈflauər] 꽃
hair [heər] 머리카락
listen [ˈlisn] 듣다
lot [laːt] 많음
parents [ˈpeərənt] 부모, 어버이

shine [ʃain] 빛나게 하다, 반짝이게 하다
shoe [ʃuː] 신발
short [ʃɔːrt] 짧은
steal [stiːl] / stole [stoul] / stolen [stouln] 훔치다
thing [θiŋ] 것(사물을 가리킴)
toy [tɔi] 장난감
wash [waʃ] 씻다, 세탁하다
work [wəːrk] 직장 / 일, 일하다

all afternoon 오후 내내
at last 마침내
buy some flowers for ~
~를 위해 꽃을 사다
have my computer fixed
내 컴퓨터를 고치다
That's because ~ 그것은 ~때문이다
this time 이번에는

해설

have 목적어(A) 과거분사 :

A가 ~을 당하다. : 목적어 A와 뒤에 오는 동사의 관계가 수동의 의미일 때 동사는 과거분사가 온다.

1) So I bought some flowers for Mary. 그래서 메리를 위해서 꽃을 샀다.
2) Do you remember what I did? 내가 한 것을 기억하니?
3) That's because I love them. 그것은 내가 그들을 사랑하기 때문이다.
4) My computer did not work well. 내 컴퓨터가 잘 작동하지 않았다.
5) So I had my computer fixed. 그래서 나는 내 컴퓨터를 고쳤다. (←컴퓨터가 고쳐짐을 당하도록 했다.)
6) I had my room cleaned. 내 방을 깨끗하게 치웠다. (← 내방이 깨끗하게 치워짐을 당하도록 했다.)
7) I had my shoes shined. 내 신발을 닦았다.
8) I had my car washed. 내차를 세차했다.
9) I had my bike stolen. 내 자전거를 도난당했다.
10) I had the bike fixed. 자전거를 수리했다.
11) I had my hair cut. I had my hair cut short. 내 머리를 잘랐다. 내 머리를 짧게 잘랐다.

(07)

Mary called me yesterday. But I was too busy. So I had her call me later.[1)] I had a lot of things to do. But I could not finish everything. I needed help. So I had Tom come.[2)] And I had him help me.[3)] I had to write a letter. So I had him write a letter.[4)] I had to clean my room. So I had him clean my room.[5)] After I finished everything that I had to do, I gave Tom some money. He was happy.

(08)

Do you want to know my plan? Okay, I'll <u>let</u> you <u>know</u> my plan.[6)] But, wait a minute please. I have to go to the bathroom right now. I will come back soon. (After a few minutes, he comes back) Hey! What are you doing now? Stop it! Stop reading my diary! I just said that I would <u>let</u> you <u>know</u> my plan.[7)] I didn't <u>let</u> you <u>see</u> my diary.[8)] I will not <u>let</u> this <u>happen</u> again.[9)] And I'll try not to <u>let</u> this <u>happen</u> again.[10)]

단어 및 숙어

again [ə'gen] 또, 다시
bathroom ['bæθrum] 화장실, 욕실
called [kɔːld] 전화하다
clean [kliːn] 청소하다 / 깨끗한
diary ['daiəri] 일기
everything ['evriθiŋ] 모든 것
explain [ik'splein] 설명하다
few [fjuː] 거의 없는, 적은 수의
finish ['finiʃ] 끝내다
guide [gaid] 안내인 / 안내하다
happen ['hæpn] 일어나다, 발생하다
ill [il] 아픈, 병든
introduce [intrə'djuːs] 소개하다
just [dʒʌst] 단지/금방
later ['leitər] 나중에
let [let] ~시키다 / ~하도록 허락하다

minute ['miniːt] 분, 순간
museum [mjuːˈziːəm] 박물관, 미술관
plan [plæn] 계획 / 계획하다
soon [suːn] 곧
try [trai] 노력하다
wait [weit] 기다리다
watch [waːtʃ] 보다

a few 어느 정도, 조금
after a few minutes 몇 분 후에
come back 돌아오다
have to ~해야만 한다
right now 지금 당장
Wait a minute please!
잠깐만 기다리세요

해설

have 목적어(A) 동사원형 : A에게 ~을 시키다.

1) I had her call me later. 나는 그녀에게 나중에 전화하게 하였다. (나중에 전화 하도록 시켰다.)
2) I had Tom come. 톰을 오게 했다. (오도록 시켰다.)
3) I had him help me. 그가 나를 돕게 했다.
4) I had him write a letter. 그가 편지를 쓰게 했다.
5) I had him clean my room. 그가 내 방을 깨끗이 치우게 했다.

사역동사 (let, make) 목적어(A) 동사원형 : A에게 ~을 시키다.

6) I'll let you know my plan. 너에게 나의 계획을 알려 줄 것이다. (← 나의 계획을 알도록 하겠다.)
7) I just said that I would let you know my plan. 나는 단지 나의 계획을 너에게 알려줄 것이라고 말했을 뿐이다.
8) I didn't let you see my diary. 나는 네가 내 일기장을 보도록 하지는 않았다.
9) I will not let this happen again. 이런 일이 다시 일어나지 않도록 하겠다.
10) And I'll try not to let this happen again. 그리고 이런 일이 다시 일어나지 않도록 노력할 것이다.

(09)

"Let me introduce myself to you.[11] My name is Minho. I'm a museum guide. I'll guide you. Let me explain this museum to you.[12] After explaining this museum, I'll show you something." He explained the museum to us. And he said, "Let me show you something."[13]

(10)

A little child got up in the morning. But he didn't want to do anything. He didn't want to wash his face. He didn't want to have breakfast. After getting up, he didn't do anything. So his mother made him brush his teeth and wash his face. After that the mother made him clean his room and made him sit at the table. And then, she mad him have breakfast.

단어 및 숙어

brush [brʌʃ] 칫솔질하다
explain [ikˈsplein] 설명하다
guide [gaid] 안내하다, 안내원
introduce [intrəˈdju:s] 소개하다
museum [mju:ˈzi:əm] 박물관
teeth [ti:θ] tooth [tu:θ] 이빨의 복수

brush his teeth 이빨을 닦다
sit at the table. 식탁에 앉다
wash his face 세수하다

해설

11) Let me introduce myself to you.
저를 소개하겠습니다. (← 제가 제 자신을 여러분들에게 소개하도록 허락해 주세요.)

12) Let me explain this museum to you.
이 박물관을 여러분들에게 설명하겠습니다. (← 제가 여러분들에게 이 박물관을 소개하도록 허락해 주세요.)

13) Let me show you something.
제가 어떤 것을 보여 드리겠습니다. (← 제가 여러분들에게 어떤 것을 보여주도록 허락해주세요.)

14) His mother made him brush his teeth and wash his face.
엄마는 양치질을 하게 하고 세수를 하게 하였다.

* 부록 : 리딩 기록표

챕터명	1회			2회			3회			4회			5회		
	분	초	이해도(%)	분	초	이해도(%)	분	초	이해도(%)	분	초	이해도(%)	분	초	이해도(%)
1장															
2장															
3장															
4장															
5장															
6장															
7장															
8장 1. 2.															
8장 3. 4.															
8장 5. 6. 7. 8. 종합이해															
9장															
10장															
11장															
12장															
13장															
14장															
15장															

챕터명	1회			2회			3회			4회			5회		
	분	초	이해도(%)	분	초	이해도(%)	분	초	이해도(%)	분	초	이해도(%)	분	초	이해도(%)
1장															
2장															
3장															
4장															
5장															
6장															
7장															
8장 1. 2.															
8장 3. 4.															
8장 5. 6. 7. 8. 종합이해															
9장															
10장															
11장															
12장															
13장															
14장															
15장															

챕터명	1회			2회			3회			4회			5회		
	분	초	이해도(%)	분	초	이해도(%)	분	초	이해도(%)	분	초	이해도(%)	분	초	이해도(%)
1장															
2장															
3장															
4장															
5장															
6장															
7장															
8장 1. 2.															
8장 3. 4.															
8장 5. 6. 7. 8. 종합이해															
9장															
10장															
11장															
12장															
13장															
14장															
15장															

챕터명	1회			2회			3회			4회			5회		
	분	초	이해도(%)	분	초	이해도(%)	분	초	이해도(%)	분	초	이해도(%)	분	초	이해도(%)
1장															
2장															
3장															
4장															
5장															
6장															
7장															
8장 1. 2.															
8장 3. 4.															
8장 5. 6. 7. 8. 종합이해															
9장															
10장															
11장															
12장															
13장															
14장															
15장															

챕터명	1회			2회			3회			4회			5회		
	분	초	이해도(%)	분	초	이해도(%)	분	초	이해도(%)	분	초	이해도(%)	분	초	이해도(%)
1장															
2장															
3장															
4장															
5장															
6장															
7장															
8장 1. 2.															
8장 3. 4.															
8장 5. 6. 7. 8. 종합이해															
9장															
10장															
11장															
12장															
13장															
14장															
15장															

챕터명	1회			2회			3회			4회			5회		
	분	초	이해도(%)	분	초	이해도(%)	분	초	이해도(%)	분	초	이해도(%)	분	초	이해도(%)
1장															
2장															
3장															
4장															
5장															
6장															
7장															
8장 1. 2.															
8장 3. 4.															
8장 5. 6. 7. 8. 종합이해															
9장															
10장															
11장															
12장															
13장															
14장															
15장															

JHO 100시간 영어 시리즈 ⑤
문법

초판 1쇄 발행 2020년 3월 17일

✚ 지은이 **JHO**

✚ 펴낸이 **이동하** ✚ 디자인 **조종완**

✚ 펴낸곳 **새잎** ✚ 등록 2010년 1월 26일 제25100-2010-0001호

✚ 서울시 중구 서울중앙우체국 사서함 3243호

✚ 전화 0505-987-4221 ✚ 팩스 0505-987-4222

ISBN: 979-11-85600-30-7 (13740)

책값은 뒤표지에 있습니다.
잘못된 도서는 구입하신 서점에서 교환해 드립니다.